Make it Happen

First published in 2011 by
Liberties Press
Guinness Enterprise Centre | Taylor's Lane | Dublin 8
Tel: +353 (1) 415 1224
www.libertiespress.com | info@libertiespress.com

Distributed in the United States by
Dufour Editions | PO Box 7 | Chester Springs | Pennsylvania | 19425

Trade enquiries to Gill & Macmillan Distribution
Hume Avenue | Park West | Dublin 12
Tel: +353 (1) 500 9534 | Fax: +353 (1) 500 9595
sales@gillmacmillan.ie

ISBN: 978-1-907593-12-3
2 4 6 8 10 9 7 5 3 1
A CIP record for this title is available from the British Library.

Cover and internal design by Ros Murphy
Printed by Castuera

Make it Happen

A Success Guide for Teenagers

Padraig Lawlor & Philip O'Callaghan

LIB
ERT
I ES

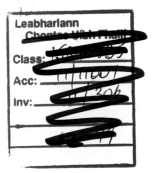

Contents

Acknowledgements

There are many people we wish to thank who helped this book become a reality. Firstly, Xanthe Wells, who provided creative direction throughout the project and assisted us in creating a book that is accessible, entertaining and engaging.

Thanks to all the contributors, who told us their personal stories of how the principles in this book helped them.

Particular thanks to Kim Jordan and Jean Walsh, two young students who proofed the material and helped us to really understand what our readers are looking for. Your advice and guidance is greatly appreciated.

To Raymond Langan, a trainer with The Super Generation, whose creative ideas and ability to communicate were invaluable in helping us distil the message of the book into understandable concepts and language. We are truly grateful for your contribution.

A special word of thanks to the many schools, teachers and young people to whom we have delivered our seminar programme. You motivated us to write this book and we hope you gain as much from it as we have from writing it.

To Sean, Clara and all the team at Liberties Press, a truly heartfelt thanks for your effort, work and patience in helping bring our vision to life.

MAKE IT HAPPEN
Why Bother?

What is success? Most people think it is about getting what you want and the faster you get it, the more successful you are. We have a different view. Success is a journey not a destination. Ultimately, success is working towards being, doing or having the things which you want in life. This book shows you how to define what success means to you and also shows you how you can achieve it.

Along our journeys of trying to be successful and finding ways to be happy, we have met many wonderful people who have helped, motivated and inspired us. We have both read many books and listened to countless stories of people who have achieved success. And that's why we've written this book: so that we can share these insights with you.

This book is a team effort. We, along with many of our friends, have contributed our ideas, knowledge and experience to create a book we hope you will both learn from and enjoy. There are plenty of personal thoughts and stories to inspire you on your journey. More importantly, we know whatever you want to achieve in life, you will find a way to do it within these pages.

It is often said that there is both an art and a science to success. We think of this book as the science, because success leaves clues. Follow the steps laid out in this book, and you are laying the foundations to succeed. There is no hidden secret to success; there is no magic formula. It is all about following some simple steps. This book will show you what those steps are, and how to follow them.

The other important thing you will learn is what we call 'the art of success'. This is the life-changing part: the art of success is the ability to enjoy the journey and be happy, no matter what the outcome. It's what we have come to understand as the real 'meaning of life'. If you can enjoy the journey, you will always be successful.

And that's the real gift. When you follow the simple steps in this book, you will discover what it is that makes you truly happy. You discover, or rather uncover, what you are passionate about, what your real purpose in life is, and what brings you joy.

There is no short cut to success: you can only uncover it as you take the journey. It is different for everyone, and may happen without you noticing it. As you travel that journey, we would be delighted if you could share your story with us. We can't promise you an easy ride, but then nothing worthwhile was ever accomplished easily. We promise you a guide, which will help you define what your personal success looks like and help you put in place the steps to achieve it. It is an invitation to start a journey like no other you will ever make.

But before you get started, we need to say one thing, and that is: 'Thank you'. Thank you for allowing us to help you on your journey. We are very passionate about helping young people. We try to do it every day, to the best of our ability. Our hope is that this book will guide you to whatever it is you want from life. We look forward to going on the journey with you.

For anyone who ever had a dream, hope or wish but didn't know how to 'make it happen', this book is for you. Good luck!

Padraig and Philip

MAKE IT HAPPEN – A Success Guide for Teenagers

User's Guide: Making **Make It Happen** Work for You

OK, so there are many different ways you can use this book. But although it could make a potential doorstop, frisbee or dinner plate, the best thing to do is to read it.

The book is divided into three sections:

1. **Introduction to Success – Episodes 1 to 4**

2. **Making It Happen – Episodes 5 to 8**

3. **The Tools for Success – Episodes 9 to 15**

The most important section is 'Making It Happen'. (Why do you think we named the book after it!). So if you want to only read a few episodes, then that's the bit for you. However, we're pretty pleased with the rest of the book too: the 'Introduction to Success' will give you information about how our minds work and what success really is, while 'The Tools for Success' will speed up your ability to make things happen. At a glance, the book looks something like this:

Make it Happen
A Success Guide
for Teenagers

Section 1
Introduction to Success

Section 2
Making it Happen
The Super System

Section 3
Tools for Success

Episode 1
It's All in the Mind
Superconscious

Episode 5
See your
Success

Episode 9
An Attitude of Gratitude
Gratitude

Episode 2
Dream Big
Imagination

Episode 6
Understand It

Episode 10
Use the Force
Affirmations

Episode 3
Break the Barriers
Empowerment

Episode 7
Plan Your Path

Episode 11
Heads or Tails
Positive Choice

Episode 4
The Secret to
Success

Episode 8
Execute and Reward

Episode 12
Team Game
Friends

Episode 13
Manage Your
Thoughts

Episode 14
Talk the Talk, Walk the Walk
Communication

Episode 15
Never Say Never
Persistence

We know that people learn in different ways, so we have used loads of different styles in this book. Like when you watch TV, you can pick and choose the bits that work best for you. You might like the step-by-step interactive features. Or you might like reading the true stories. Alternatively, you might be a channel-hopper and only read the fictional stories and the 'ad breaks'. If one of these sounds like you, then that's fine. And if there are sections that really don't suit you, then don't worry: just take what you need from the book. We recommend a quick dip into the book to get a sense of what it's about from the bits you like, before you sit down to read it properly. But, like any TV series, it always helps to start at the beginning and keep going, episode by episode, until you reach the end. After that, you can revisit your favourite episodes as much and as often as you like.

Like watching TV, you can pick and choose the bits you want.

Of course, you could have a back-to-back episode marathon and read the whole thing in one go. The important thing is that you use this book as a manual that you can refer back to whenever you want.

At the beginning of each episode is the 'TV listing' for that particular episode, showing where it fits into the schedule and what the episode is about. You can use these to help you navigate through the book and to plan what bits you might want to return to in the future. Stick markers in it, highlight bits, and write your comments and thoughts in it wherever you like.

Finally, this is an interactive book, so every now and again we'll ask you to 'Press The Red Button' and get interactive with a short activity. You can write your notes in the space provided in the book, but you might like to get a notebook to keep all your thoughts together so that you can revisit them and add to them later. Some of the exercises should ideally be done every day, but don't worry, we don't expect you to tackle all of them at once. The idea of the book is that it becomes a guide to use along your way to success, so there's no rush. Just do the exercises that are right for you at the time. You may find you come back to others later on, maybe days, weeks, months or even years from now.

Here are some descriptions of the main features you should look out for:

▶ Now and Next ⎔

At the beginning of each episode, this handy schedule tells you what's going on in the episode. Use it to give you an overview of what's to come and to help you find the sections you want to go back to in the future.

Channel Hop

This symbol shows we have changed subject or style, as if you've changed channel to another programme. Just like you can get bored of a TV show and want to see what else is on, Channel Hop sections spice up the book and keep you interested!

Reality Bite

These sections contain the real stories of real people. Yes, really! We think they are important to show you what we are talking about really can make things happen – and will make things happen for you.

Tech Specs

Sometimes it's useful to know the science behind the subject. Tech Spec does just that – without too much jargon.

Press the Red Button ▶

Here you can go interactive and get stuck in to techniques and exercises that will help you get the most out of this book. Remember, you don't have to do all of them at once. Page 8 has all the Red Button exercises in the book listed, for you to record which ones you've done and how you got on.

Press Pause

Press pause, and take some time to think about what's been said and how it relates to you.

Replay

You've seen this one at work already. Some things are so good they're worth saying twice! These snippets are the really important bits that will help you to Make it Happen.

Listen Up

These are short quotations that summarise a particular idea or concept. Read all of these, and you'll be on the way to success without even trying!

60 Seconds

At the end of each episode, we give you a quick roundup of all the important bits of the episode. This way, you can refresh your memory before you head on through the book. You can also use them as quick reminders when you come back to the book in the future.

So that's the basics covered. Now let's start making it happen!

Exercises

Use this table to help you keep a note of which exercises you have done and which ones you would like to do next. Use the comments sections to make a note of your first impressions, and compare them when you revisit the exercises again later. You may be surprised at the change in your perception!

Episode	Page	Title	Done	Comments
1		Limiting beliefs		
2		What is success?		
		Motivation		
		Wheel of life		
3		Create empowering beliefs		
		Self-image		
5		Write your Personal Vision Statement		

Episode	Page	Title	Done	Comments
14		Good Impressions and Rapport		
		Mirroring		
		Power language		
15		Develop your persistence		

Make it Happen
A Success Guide for Teenagers

Section 1
Introduction to Success

Section 2
Making it Happen
The Super System

Section 3
Tools for Success

Episode 1
It's All in the Mind
Superconscious

Episode 2
Dream Big
Imagination

Episode 3
Break the Barriers
Empowerment

Episode 4
The Secret to
Success

Episode 5
See your Success

Episode 6
Understand It

Episode 7
Plan The Path

Episode 8
Execute and Reward

Episode 9
An Attitude of Gratitude
Gratitude

Episode 10
Use the Force
Affirmations

Episode 11
Heads or Tails
Positive Choice

Episode 12
Team Game
Friends

Episode 13
Manage Your
Thoughts

Episode 14
Talk the Talk, Walk the Walk
Communication

Episode 15
Never Say Never
Persistence

▶ Now and Next 📺

NOW It's All in the mind – How your mind works and how to get your superconsclous to work for you.

NEXT Dream Big – Imagining your route to success

There is a very important piece of kit you need to have in order to make things happen. It is the ultimate in processing technology: better, faster and smarter than the most expensive computer in the shops today. But don't despair. Before you start moaning about the fact that you'll never be able to afford such an amazing machine, we'll let you into a secret: you already have it.

'Wow, thanks Mum and Dad, it's just what I've always wanted! '

NEW MIND on sale at all good stockists

This fantastic piece of equipment is, you've guessed it, your *mind*. And the good news is that we all have one (although some of us use it more than others). But what we want to share with you is how our mind works and how it affects what we think and do. Once you know these two things, there will be no stopping you on your journey to making your life a success!

Horror TV

The lightning shot down onto the tower and lit up the room. Dr X laughed manically as she threw the lever that connected the power surge to her creations. The room crackled with electricity, and the smell of burning drifted into the damp Transylvanian air.

From the table in the centre of the room came a low groan. And then another. Two figures slowly sat upright and turned to face their creator.

'Aaaaha ha ha haa,' she cackled gleefully. 'You are alive my precious ones.'

'Am I?' asked one.

'Of course,' replied the other. 'Our new state has been instigated by the electrical current coursing through our constructed limbs to connect our synapses, restart our hearts and send the source of life into our very bodies.'

'But I don't feel alive,' the first one said.

'Feelings are irrelevant,' answered the second. 'We are alive because we are. I think therefore I am.'

'But I have to feel. I have to believe in something. If I have nothing to believe in, then I cannot exist.' Saying this, the first creation disappeared.

'I cannot understand that,' said the second creation. 'If I cannot understand, I cannot exist.' And he too vanished.

Dr X looked forlornly at the table where her two amazing creatures had been.

'I knew I shouldn't have split one brain between the two of them,' she said.

Our minds are made up of two parts: the thinking mind and the feeling mind, or the *conscious* and the *superconscious* mind.

The Conscious Mind

Now, no doubt you will have heard this term before. In fact, you probably use it in your day-to-day vocabulary. For example:

'I was conscious of the time, so I went home quickly.'

Or: 'I was so tired in that lesson, I was barely conscious.'

We use it to mean 'thinking about' or 'aware' or even 'awake'. By contrast, when we are asleep (or have received a large blow to the head) we are said to be *unconscious*.

So it makes sense for us to use the term 'the conscious mind' to refer to that part of ourselves which is in control of thinking, doing and making decisions.

Conscious
Thinking

Superconscious
Feeling

The conscious mind is in control of thinking, doing and making decisions.

This can make the conscious mind sound really important and significant, but in fact it doesn't have as much impact as we think. You see, the conscious mind is only the outer appearance of the mind. Holding the power, but hiding in the shadows, is the 'superconscious mind'.

The Superconscious Mind

We use the term 'the superconscious mind' to mean the part of ourselves that holds all the unseen information that we use without even thinking. It's also known as the 'subconscious mind', and is often thought of as the 'feeling' part of a person.

The superconscious mind holds all the unseen information that we use without even thinking about it.

Our superconscious is like an enormous warehouse, holding everything we have thought, seen or done in our life so far. It's always working, and uses about 90 percent of our total brain power.

This is what makes the superconscious so *super*. Without us knowing, it's working out how we feel, what we remember, and what we

MAKE IT HAPPEN – A Success Guide for Teenagers

believe. Amazingly, it lets us concentrate on the exciting bits and bobs of life, while it does all the other stuff automatically. Think about it for a moment. When did you last have to remember to blink your eyes? Or think about how to walk? Or how to brush your teeth, tie your shoelaces or use a computer mouse? Of course, you've had to learn how to do all of these things at some stage in your life, but once you've worked out how to do them, you can sit back and let your superconscious take control. Marvellous!

Press Pause ⏸

Imagine your favourite celebrity. It could be a rock star, an actor, a comedian . . . Got a picture of them in your mind? OK. Now look to the left or right of them. Who's that person who's always just a few paces away from them? That's right, their bodyguard.

Now imagine it's late at night and the celebrity wants to go into the city and have a meal. The bodyguard may prefer to go to bed but, because it's his job, he accompanies the celeb to the restaurant. When they pull up outside, there's a huge commotion from the public, and a crazy fan tries to throw herself on their favourite celeb. What happens? If the bodyguard is any good, they will instantly move to protect the celebrity. Whatever the situation – whether the crazy fan wants to get an autograph or to attack – it's the bodyguard's job to act without thinking to protect them. That's what they've been trained to do.

In much the same way, the conscious mind thinks and makes decisions (like where to go and what to do) while the superconscious does what it has been trained to do (breathe, walk, and so on). Now this is undoubtedly very handy and useful but, because the superconscious can't think or make decisions, it can be trained to do stuff that the conscious mind hasn't stopped to think about. These become habits, and these habits become our belief system. The more we do something, the more our mind believes that this is the right thing to do (even when it isn't), and it will keep telling us to follow that action. It's how we remember to do positive things, like brush our teeth every day, and how we get caught up doing negative things, like biting our nails. Luckily, we can change our beliefs with a bit of help from our superconscious.

Our belief system is the foundation on which we build our behaviour. It acts as a filter between our conscious and our superconscious: it's the jam in our mind sandwich, if you will. Whatever we feel or experience in our superconscious forms a belief, and the conscious mind then uses these beliefs to help us understand ourselves and the world around us.

Our belief system acts as a filter between our conscious and our superconscious.

Replay ↻

History Today

- Before the fourth century BC, people believed that the world was flat. This made sense: you could see to the flat line of the horizon, therefore the earth *must* be flat.
- By 330 BC, the Greek philosopher and scientist Aristotle had provided evidence that the world was a sphere. What a weird idea, people thought.
- By the eighth century AD, it was commonly accepted that the world was indeed a sphere. This made sense: however far you went, you didn't fall off the edge.
- In nineteenth-century England, some Christian thinkers began to argue that the world was, in fact, flat. What a weird idea, people thought.
- In 1968, the crew of the Apollo 8 Moon mission took a photograph of the Earth from the Moon's orbit. It was a blue sphere. Well, that proves that the world is round, people thought.
- Today, there are thousands of people across the globe (or disc, depending on your point of

view) who believe that the world is actually flat. They are known as 'flat-earthers'. (If you don't believe us, look 'em up.) They believe that the Moon landing was a hoax and that the photographic evidence for it was faked. What a weird idea, people thought. Or is it?

The thing about our beliefs is not whether or not they are true, but the fact that our superconscious *believes* them to be true. This is the scary bit: if our superconscious *believes* something to be true, our conscious will *make* it true. So if we can learn how to slip our superconscious some really great beliefs about our lives, just think what we could achieve!

'Whether you believe you can, or whether you believe you can't – you're right.'

Henry Ford, of the Ford Motor Company

Self-Limiting Beliefs

Many of our beliefs are useful, and prevent us from harm: for example, a fire will burn you, and stepping out in front of a car could kill you. However, some of the beliefs we have don't serve us so well. We call these 'self-limiting' beliefs, because they prevent us from achieving our potential.

Self-limiting beliefs prevent us from achieving our potential.

As you work your way through this book, there will be time to look at your belief system and give it a spring-clean by dusting off your positive beliefs and throwing out the old, negative ones. We will even give you some techniques to develop new beliefs which will support and empower you as you begin to make things happen.

Aged nine, I was in the school choir along with all my classmates. We were preparing to perform in front of our parents for a Christmas concert. However, my teacher didn't think that I had a singing voice and asked me not to sing, but to mime the words instead. She said that nobody would notice. Maybe that was true, but I certainly did. She planted a belief in me that I was unable to sing; this affected my self-confidence and my own perception of my singing ability. For a number of years, I firmly held the belief that I was unable to sing, and always refused to sing in front of people, even though I would have dearly loved to do so.

I was lucky. In sixth class, I had a teacher that held a different belief: indeed, he believed that everyone could sing, and was determined to show me that I could too. He spent a lot of time singing with us and was always enthusiastic about the annual folk mass. I believed that I was tone-deaf, but he refused to accept this. He got me to sing simple songs as part of a group; eventually, after a lot of work, he proved to me that I could sing. He was proud of his achievement, and I was delighted to be proved wrong: I really loved to sing, but I was too shy to admit it. Finally, I sang as part of a duet in our sixth-class folk mass in the local church. I was delighted with myself.

Sarah's teacher worked hard to change a disempowering belief which she had been given in early life. No doubt the junior teacher was well intentioned, but Sarah's superconscious mind was not able to distinguish between fact and fiction, and in this case it accepted the negative false beliefs that the teacher had given her. If she had not encountered another, extraordinary teacher, she would still be living with those negative beliefs today.

Sarah works as a housewife in Wicklow and still enjoys singing in the local church.

Limiting Beliefs

Take a moment to think about the things that you believe you can't do. Write them down. You might have one or two, or lots of them.

Now look at your list and, for each one, ask yourself: where did I learn to believe the belief that I can't . . . ?
Think right back, and try to remember the time you were first told you couldn't do something.
Was it as a baby? A toddler? At school?
Who helped you 'construct' your belief? Your parents? Relatives? Friends? (We call people who sow the seeds of self-limiting beliefs, 'dreambusters'; there's more on them coming up in Episode 2.)
If you can find these memories in your superconscious, write them down. If you can't quite catch them, don't worry: they'll come to you when you least expect it – such is the power of the superconscious!

Your Notes!

So, where do your self-limiting beliefs come from? Once you can answer this question, you're well on the way to turning your limiting beliefs into empowering ones.

Empowering Beliefs

As we've already said, the superconscious mind is a clever piece of kit. As children, before our conscious mind develops, we only have our superconscious. This is why, when you tell a small child about Santa Claus or the Tooth Fairy, they believe you. It's also why, if you give your four-year-old cousin a lemon and tell them it'll taste nice, they'll believe you – although you may not want to face the consequences of actually trying that out!

But the best bit about the superconscious is not just that it *forms* our beliefs, but that it lets us *act* on them as well. And positive actions bring positive results.

Positive actions bring positive results.

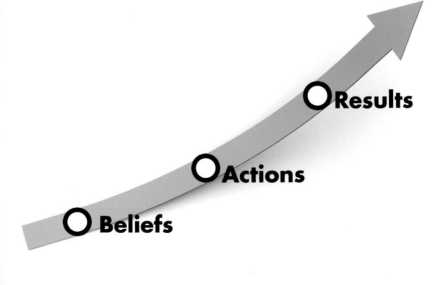

For example, if you tell a child that they are fantastic at swimming, they will believe that they are fantastic at swimming. This makes them act as though they are a fantastic swimmer and, lo and behold, they become the best swimmers they can be.

Tech Specs

In the same way, if you go to the doctor and she gives you some tablets to make you feel better, you believe those tablets will make you feel better – even if you find out later that she's actually given you sugar pills. This is known as the placebo effect. Scientists have proven in many cases of illness and disease that a placebo can have a positive effect on the patient. This shows that it's not only the medicine but also the superconscious mind's belief that helps alleviate pain and illness.

So it's true: what we achieve in life is directly due to our beliefs. Impressive, or what?

Ben Underwood was born in Riverside, California, on 26 January 1992. At the age of two, he was diagnosed with bilateral retnoblastoma (cancer in both eyes). Ben's tumour was a very slow-growing one, but his condition was still very serious.

Ben's right eye was completely consumed by the cancer, so it was removed. After that, he had another eight months of chemo, and then six weeks of radiation therapy, to try to save the left eye. These treatments were unsuccessful.
Ben's mother had to make a tough decision for her child. Of course, she would do anything to keep him alive, and agreed to have his second eye removed.

When Ben woke up after the surgery, he said: 'Mom, I can't see any more. Oh mom, I can't see.' But instead of Ben's mother letting him feel her fears, she said: 'Ben, you can still see.'

She took his little hands and put them on her face and said: 'See me. You can see me with your hands.' Next, she put her hand to his nose and said: 'Smell me. You can see me with your nose.' Then she said: 'Hear me. You can see me with your ears. You can't use your eyes any more, but you have your hands, your nose and your ears.' Ben has been seeing ever since.

His mother treated him as though he could see, and used visual language with him. She made sure that he 'saw' everything. She would put his hand on the road and say: 'Look at this: the road is rough, and the sidewalk is smooth.' You name it, she put his hand on it.

Soon afterwards, Ben started using clicking noises to help him 'see' even better. Ben says he practiced, to see how far his echo would go. He could hear a rubbish bin on the floor, and could work out where stationary objects were. He was able to play video games, ride a bike, skate, climb trees – do everything he always had done, as if he had never lost his sight.

When his doctor saw Ben playing his Game Boy, he was amazed. He walked into the patient room and looked at Ben, walked over to the computer desk and looked into his chart, walked back over to Ben and looked in his eyes, then looked down to see if he was really playing the game. He finally looked over to Ben's mother and said: 'His eyes are nucleated.' She said: 'Oh yes, he's blind.' The doctor said: 'How the heck does he play video games?' She replied: 'He does everything: ride bikes, rollerblades, electric scooters. You name it, he will try it.'

Ben started writing a novel when he was in fourth grade. He writes at the level of a college student, and types at a speed of about sixty words a minute on a regular keyboard. His novel is science fiction; he has written at least twenty chapters. He also wants to develop video games. He is so full of ideas, and he is encouraged to pursue them all.

His mother says: 'The sky is the limit, and you can accomplish anything you set your mind to if you try. Don't stress about failure, because success often begins from there. The only place from rock bottom is up, and failure is bottom.'

Sadly, Ben's cancer returned, and he died, aged sixteen, on 19 January 2009. Ben may have only had a short life, but it was certainly a full one. You can read the complete story at www.benunderwood.com.

Ben's story truly shows the power of belief. If his mum had given him a white stick or a guide dog, he might never have developed his 'sight' in the incredible way he did. Instead, through the power of the superconscious mind's acceptance that he could see, he was able to participate in the world as much as anyone else.

Chain Reaction

Our beliefs trigger a chain reaction from thought to result. That reaction can be either positive or negative. For instance:

I'm no good at maths'

If you are told you are no good at maths, and you believe that you are no good at it, your feelings towards the subject will be negative. This will make you not want to do your homework (because it won't help), and you won't study for your exams (because you know you won't pass). These negative actions will result in negative results – your chances of passing are greatly reduced.

'I am good at maths'

If, on the other hand, you think you are good at maths and receive positive reinforcement from others, you feel positive towards it. This makes you want to work harder and study more...these positive actions result in positive results and your success!

It's pretty obvious that positive thoughts and feelings are better in the long run than negative ones. But wait, here comes the science bit . . .

MAKE IT HAPPEN – A Success Guide for Teenagers

Our brains are made up of billions of cells with 'arms' called dendrites. Each dendrite is separated from the others by tiny spaces called 'synaptic gaps'. When you have a thought, it sparks an impulse in the centre (nucleus) of the dendrite, which speeds off along the arms to make a connection with another dendrite. When this happens, the thought spreads out across your brain cells to form a pattern of understanding.

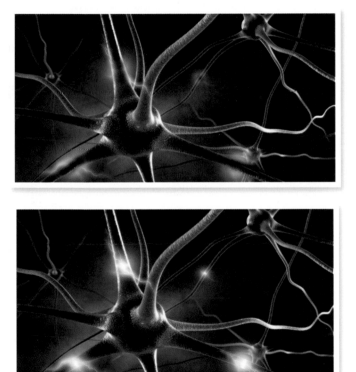

But this is the clever part: if you have a positive thought, the impulse releases a chemical called serotonin at the end of the dendrite arm. Not only does this give you feelings of happiness and well-being, but it also allows the thought to bridge the synaptic gap and spread out across your mind: it makes good things happen, if you like.

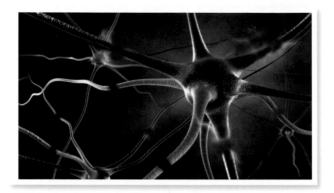

On the other hand, if you have a negative thought, the chemical cortisone is released. This makes you feel sad and miserable and, more importantly, it blocks the gap and prevents the thoughts from becoming positive: it actually *stops* good things from happening.

So, thinking empowering thoughts allows a free flow of ideas, so that good things can happen. Thinking self-limiting thoughts prevents this flow, and means that you only see more problems and dilemmas. Isn't science great?

(For more about this, read *Goal Mapping* by Brian Mayne.)

Reality Bite

Michelle's parents were neither wealthy nor privileged. Her father worked at a city water plant; her mother was a full-time homemaker. Michelle's family history didn't hold much success either, with ancestors on both sides of her family coming from American slavery.

But that didn't mean that the family did not believe in success. Quite the opposite, in fact. Michelle's father had multiple sclerosis, but living with a limp and having to use crutches did not deter him from being the family's bread-winner. Nor did issues of race and colour.

The couple their children that they could succeed despite

any prejudices that they may encounter in life. They also taught them that achievement and hard work would bring them the success they deserved.

Michelle did face discrimination as she progressed through her education: she was part of a programme for gifted students in her first school and went on to become one of the very few black students attending Princeton University. She was even dissuaded by the college counsellors at Harvard from studying law. Thankfully, Michelle's self-belief carried her through Harvard and on to a position in a top Chicago law firm. Here she met her future husband, Barack Obama.

As the wife of the president of the United States, Michelle Obama still believes in the importance of striving to achieve success. She is in bed most nights by half past nine and rises each morning at half past four, to run on a treadmill. She still believes what her parents taught her: 'You work hard for what you want in life, your word is your bond, and you do what you say you're going to do.'

Channel Hop

Computing for You

Our body is like a computer system, with its own hardware and software. Our body is the hardware – the machine, if you like – and our beliefs are the software. Computers are not much use without software, and most of them come pre-programmed with an operating system. Our operating system of beliefs is often pre-installed by people who want the best for us (like our parents); then we go through life adding software to help us develop along the way.

Sometimes, the software we have doesn't help us move forward, but contains limiting beliefs lurking inside, like viruses. If your computer gets a virus, you can often still use it for a while, but eventually the virus starts to corrupt your other programmes, and the computer begins to malfunction. If the virus penetrates your operating system, it may be too late, and your computer will respond only with the blank screen of death. Even switching it off and on again won't help!

If this happens, the only solution is to wipe out your software and reinstall everything, including the operating system. Some people use this opportunity to choose a more appropriate operating system. Others are happy just to reinstall the bits they need. After having a bad experience with a virus, people are generally more cautious about what software they accept and will install an antivirus package and firewall to help protect them from dangerous programmes or viruses in the future.

If we approach our beliefs with the same care and attention that we use when we accept or decline email attachments, we can monitor whether we are accepting empowering or limiting beliefs. We can perform virus scans with tools and exercises, and we can reject negative thoughts – even from those who want the best for us. In short, we can keep our hardware safe and allow it to run at optimum capacity.

So that's Episode 1. You made it! Take a break – maybe grab a cup of tea and some biscuits – then get stuck into Episode 2, where we'll tell you all about success, and how you can make it a reality.

It's all in the mind

1. Our minds are made up of the *conscious* 'thinking' mind and the *superconscious* 'feeling' mind.

2. Our *belief system* acts as a filter between our conscious and our superconscious.

3. What our superconscious believes to be true, our conscious will act upon.

4. Self-limiting beliefs prevent us from getting positive results by convincing us that we are not good enough, or not able enough, to do something.

5. *Empowering* beliefs help us to believe in our abilities and to achieve success.

6. Our beliefs set up a *chain reaction* of **thoughts ⇨ feelings ⇨ actions ⇨ results**.

7. It has been scientifically proven that *positive thoughts* make you feel good and help you to achieve, while *negative thoughts* make you feel low, and more likely to give up.

8. By becoming more aware of our thoughts and feelings, and using tools to help us, we can create new beliefs and *achieve success*!

Up Next . . . Dream Big: Your ideas about success

Episode 2:
Dream Big

▶ Now and Next 📺

NOW	**Dream Big: What success is, what it means to you, and how to keep your life in balance.**
NEXT	**Break the Barriers: What's standing in the way of your dreams?**

We've talked about the way in which limiting beliefs can affect our lives by holding us back and preventing us from being successful. In this episode, we're going to imagine stepping outside those limiting beliefs. Suddenly anything is possible. Now you can 'dream the impossible dream'.

But we're not going to stop there. Remember the superconscious, and its ability to turn beliefs into actions, and then into results? Well, guess what? Your superconscious can help you make things happen – however unlikely that may seem to you.

Hey 'cuz I believe in me
If I can see it then I can do it
If I just believe it, there's nothing to it

> R. Kelly, from his hit song 'I Believe I Can Fly'

Permission to Dream

When we are children, we think we can be anything 'when we grow up'. We could be a teacher, an astronaut or, if we really wanted, a caterpillar, like Ralph from *The Simpsons*: 'When I grow up, I want to be a principal or a caterpillar.'

Because we don't use our conscious mind until we are a bit older, it doesn't

MAKE IT HAPPEN – A Success Guide for Teenagers

occur to us that some of these things might be harder to achieve than others. Then, as we grow up, we begin to realise the outer world puts things in the way of our dreams. For example, you might be told that you're not clever enough to be a doctor, or you can't be an artist because they don't make much money. All these things seem to make sense because they fit with our growing beliefs about the world. And so, before you know it, you believe that you can't be a doctor or an artist, and you give up trying.

But what if you really *could* do whatever you wanted? How great would that feel!

Reality Bite

James was studying for his final exams. He worked hard at school and at the local pizza parlour in the evenings and at weekends. He deserved to do well at whatever he decided to do, but he just couldn't decide what he wanted to do. On the one hand, he wanted to go to university and get a degree, but on the other hand he thought it might be better if he got a job. When we talked to James about his options, he revealed a host of self-limiting beliefs, such as:

'If I go to university, I still might not get a job.'

'I ought to read law and become a solicitor, because that's what's expected of me.'

'I don't want to get into debt.'

'I want to be able to drive my car, but I won't be able to if I'm at university.'

'People think that media studies is a rubbish subject.'

James certainly had a lot on his mind; it's easy to see how it was so difficult for him to make his decision. Every time he tried to think about university and what course he could do, all the negative thoughts jumped in and blocked his thought patterns, making him feel that everything was too hard.

However, when James was encouraged to step outside of his self-

limiting beliefs, he was able to answer this question: if you could do anything, what would it be? James didn't even hesitate: he wanted to be an extreme-sports photographer.

So what was stopping him?
He didn't have a camera – but he could save up and buy one. He didn't have a degree – but he could go to university and get one. Suddenly, James's initial problem, of what to do after his exams, was solved. He knew what he wanted and, more importantly, he knew that there was no reason why he couldn't make it happen.
James is now studying for his final exams before he goes on to further study.

So never be afraid to set your sights on your ultimate goal. This book is about creating young leaders, not followers. We want to inspire you to recognise your uniqueness and your strengths, so that you can identify the life you want to live and then move forward with certainty and determination to achieve your goals. Whatever your self-limiting beliefs, you always have permission to dream. Permission to be creative. Permission to reflect on your life, and find out exactly what it is you want. And whatever you want to do, or be, or have, we respect that. And so must you.

Listen Up

'Never be afraid to play a big game.'
　　Julie Starr, author of The Coaching Manual and Brilliant Coaching

Defining Success

What is meant by the term 'success'? Everyone wants success, but we don't always know how to define it. Some people want money or power, while others want to start a family or to help in the community. One person may not feel that they are a success until they have invented a cure for cancer; someone else may feel that they are a success by waking up every morning with a smile on their face.

MAKE IT HAPPEN – A Success Guide for Teenagers

What Is Success?

Next time you're with a group of people – family, friends, football supporters – ask them what success means to them. If you can, write down their answers. Later, look at your list. How many definitions are there? Do they have anything in common?

Your Notes!

Success Defined

There are many different ways to describe success, how can we create a general definition?

Well, in true cookery-programme tradition . . . here's one we made earlier:

Success is working towards what you want to be, do or have

Because we believe that success is a journey not a destination, it is the working towards your goals that makes you a success. Once you decide what it is you want to be, do or have and start working towards it, then you are already a success. Failure therefore, only happens when you give up. You are still successful even if you have some setbacks, as long as you continue to work towards what it is you want.

*Mountain climbing was not something I ever thought I would be able to do. I had seen and heard stories about the great climbers and their amazing feats, and thought that this was not something that an ordinary person could do. At least, that **used** to be my belief.*

When I was travelling through South America, I set myself the challenge of completing a mountain climb. Cotopaxi in Ecuador was a truly monster climb, of 5,897 metres. It was a snow climb too, which made it even more difficult. Reaching the summit of the mountain became my goal. When I stood on top of that mountain, I would be successful.

When I started the climb, all was well. But shortly after leaving base camp, I began to feel the effects of altitude sickness. I had terrible nausea and stomach cramps, as well as headaches and general fatigue. The only way to stop altitude sickness getting worse is to return to a lower altitude. But I had a goal: I wasn't about to turn back so soon after I'd started.

The symptoms got worse: after about three hours climbing, I had to stop about every half an hour because of the stomach cramps: I'd be doubled over on the side of the mountain, wincing in pain. But I pushed on regardless. The cramps got worse, until I was stopping every twenty minutes, then every fifteen, then every ten.

At one point, I lost a glove. I dropped it while I was taking a drink. I watched as it bounced down a seventy-degree incline into the white, snowy depths below. At the time, I wasn't overly upset about losing the glove, but I soon realise how important it is to have good equipment when you're climbing. The cold wasn't the worst; the wind chill really made things tough for me. To keep my hands warm, I would transfer the one glove I had left from hand to hand every ten minutes or so. This helped a bit but eventually I lost the feeling in the tops of my fingers. (I didn't get the feeling back fully until three months after the climb.). All this just added to the torture I was going through.

About an hour and a half from the summit, we stopped for a break. My guide looked at me and asked if I was OK. (He later

told me that he was considering taking me off the mountain at that point.) But when he asked me that question, something flipped in my mind.

I wasn't OK – he could see that clearly – but I looked at him, and said the following words in such a way that he knew I meant them: 'I will get to the f**king top.' And when I said it, something happened in my mind. I had been almost ready to give up. I really didn't want to be on that mountain. I knew that the minute I starting going down, I would begin to feel better, but something stopped me from doing it.

From that moment on, I knew I would make it. All I could see in my mind was a picture of myself standing on top of the mountain. The only words I said were: 'I will get to the f**king top.' I said it out loud; I think my guide thought I had gone a little mad! I took step after step, repeating the words over and over, like a mantra. The vision was clear in my mind.

It's impossible to describe how I felt but, even though I was in the worst pain I had ever experienced, I didn't think about it. The only thought in my mind was getting to the top of that mountain.

And then finally, after seven hours of walking, I stood on top of Mount Cotopaxi. I looked around, but because of the blizzard, there wasn't much of a view. You could just about see the hand in front of your face. I stood there, cold, wet, tired, sick and hungry, and said to myself: 'Is this it? Is this success?'

Then I realised that standing there, having conquered the

mountain, was not success. Success was every step I'd taken along the way. Success was overcoming my fears. Success was battling beyond what I thought were my limits. 'Success is working towards what you want to be, do or have.' I finally understood what those words meant. It's great to have goals, and it's wonderful when you achieve them, but true success is how you develop as a person along the way.

Even if I hadn't made it to the top of the mountain, I was still a success. I had set myself a target, worked hard to achieve it, and learned a lot about myself in the process. The success was the journey.

Padraig is lead trainer and managing director of
The Super Generation

Triumph Over Adversity

If success is a journey towards your dream, there are bound to be some barriers along the way. But don't let that faze you. Countless people across the world have achieved their dreams against the odds – whether the problems they faced were lack of money or education, or tragic life events. The key is never to let anything stand in your way.

Reality Bite

Eighteen-year-old Scott Rigsby was riding in the back of a pickup truck with his friends after a day's work. Then tragedy struck: a juggernaut crashed into the truck and pulled Scott under its wheels. He was dragged underneath the trailer for three hundred metres.

Scott lost his right leg in the accident and suffered third-degree burns. After more than a decade spent in and out of hospital, he had to have his left leg amputated.

Life didn't seem too good to Scott. He struggled with an addiction to prescription pain-relieving medications, struggled with relationships, and ended up broke and despondent after selling his furniture to pay his rent. Finding a dream seemed like a tall order.

Then, in 2005, Scott decided to change his life and become an inspiration rather than a failure. He wanted to break down the barriers for physically challenged athletes – and along the way, inspire countless able-bodied people too.

Scott's dream is to make a difference. And on his journey to achieving that dream, he has achieved the unthinkable: he took part in thirteen triathlons and five road races before setting world records for a double below-the-knee amputee in the full marathon, half Ironman and international distance triathlon. Not one for stopping, Scott decided to complete the full Ironman – over sixteen hours of gruelling physical activity, with 2.4 miles of ocean swimming, 112 miles of cycling, and finally a full marathon, in the dark.

Not an easy task, but then Scott was no stranger to adversity. He coped with the ordeals of nature, prosthetics, and an allergy to hotel linen so that he could achieve his dream of crossing the finish line.

But for Scott, there is no finish line. He consistently achieves his goals, and will continue to do so – whatever life may throw at him.

For more about Scott Rigsby's remarkable story, check out
www.scottrigsby.com

Channel Hop

Characteristics of Success

As long as there has been success, there have been people trying to work out what exactly it is, and how to achieve it. By studying successful people, we have found shared goals and characteristics that can be applied in any walk of life. Here are our top eight:

Success Awards

The nominees for characteristics that successful people have in common are:

1. Having a dream, passion or purpose
2. Enthusiasm and motivation
3. Hard work
4. Planning and doing
5. Persistence

6. Good people skills

7. Specific knowledge or training

8. Being grateful for their life

And the winner is . . .

Having a dream, passion or purpose

Without a dream or goal to aim for, success is much harder to achieve. It's like setting off for a walk and not knowing where you're going. Sure, you will end up somewhere, but without a destination in mind, or a map to direct you, it could easily be somewhere you don't want to go – or you could even up right back where you started.

Replay 🔄

Without a dream or goal to aim for, success is much harder to find.

People who achieve success usually know exactly where they are going, and how they are going to get there. They have planned their route to the top of the mountain, packed their sandwiches and laced up their walking boots. If they get caught in a thunderstorm, or their path is blocked by a fallen tree, their perseverance and determination to arrive at the top will ensure that they don't give up and go home. And when they reach the top of the mountain, they will be amazed by the view, but they will also be proud of the climb, and the experience of getting there.

Press the Red Button ▶

Motivation

One of the characteristics of successful people is being motivated. How motivated are you? Ask yourself the following questions, and jot down your answers.

On a scale of 1 to 10 (where 1 is 'Can't even be bothered' and 10 is 'Nothing's gonna stop me'), how motivated would you be to do the following? Circle the number you think fits best.

a) Jump off a cliff?	1 2 3 4 5 6 7 8 9 10
b) Run a marathon?	1 2 3 4 5 6 7 8 9 10
c) Read two hundred books?	1 2 3 4 5 6 7 8 9 10
d) Do a bungee jump?	1 2 3 4 5 6 7 8 9 10

e) Learn to play the piano?   1 2 3 4 5 6 7 8 9 10
f) Rescue a loved one from a burning building?   1 2 3 4 5 6 7 8 9 10

How did you score? Does your motivation level change depending on the task? Why? Would you be more motivated to do some tasks than others?

Extremely successful people demonstrate high levels of motivation on a daily basis. They are capable of this because everything they do is a step towards their ultimate dream: the thing they are most motivated to achieve. Their motivation levels never waver: that's what makes them able to keep going, and keep striving to achieve, even when they are faced with difficulties. Imagine approaching everything with the same motivation that you would if you had to rescue someone from a potentially life-threatening situation: think how much you could get done!

Highly successful people demonstrate high levels of motivation on a daily basis.

Taking Stock

Before we can decide what we want to achieve in life, we have to assess our starting position. It's no good trying to climb a mountain if you're not physically fit enough to do so. Think about it: if you haven't done any training, the odds of you making it even halfway up will be pretty slim.

Being a teenager (or an adult, for that matter) can be a bit like that. When you're busy, it's easy to let things go. For example, if you're busy at school with exams, for example, you might not spend time visiting Gran or learning to play the guitar. This is OK every now and then, but what if your dream is to be a professional guitarist? How are you going to achieve this if you don't practise?

When we don't pay enough attention to the things that are important to us, we say that our life is 'off balance': we are usually looking too much in one direction. Sometimes it helps to take a moment or two to look at how our life is at the moment, and to consider how we would like it to be altered so that it comes into balance, enabling us to do everything in a more even way. We do this using a tool called 'the Wheel of Life'.

The Wheel of Life

The Wheel of Life gives us an overview of what we spend our time and energy on, and allows us to make changes to help our life be more in balance. By highlighting the areas in your life that are out of balance, you can discover which areas you need to focus on. You can then link this to your goals for future success, so that our life can be more well-rounded. Like the wheels on a bike being under-inflated, if your wheel of life is uneven, your journey will be bumpy and uncomfortable. This can cause stress and frustration, and throw up a range of negative beliefs, which will hinder your route to achievement.

TOUGH TYRES

GIVING YOU THE
PERFECT BALANCE

How does it work?

Each area of life that is important to you is mapped onto a circle – with each area representing one 'spoke' of the wheel. You then mark on each spoke how content you are with that area of your life: 'completely content' is the rim of wheel, while 'not at all happy' is the hub of the wheel. When you join up the marks on each spoke, you can see how you are balancing the important things in your life.

This teenager's life is out of balance. Looking at their wheel, we can learn several things. They spend a lot of time and energy on school work. They are having lots of fun, and spending time with friends, but feel that they don't have enough time with their family. They are also not too happy with their health: maybe all the fun they are having is taking its toll on them physically?
You can put anything you want on

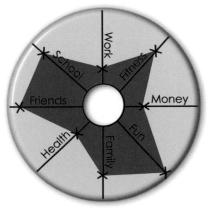

your wheel of life: everyone has a different view of what's important to them. Here are our favourites on the wheel of life, to get you started:

1. **Health and fitness**
2. **Relationships (family, friends, boyfriend/girlfriend)**
3. **Wealth and finances**
4. **Career and work**
5. **Education and growth (learning new skills or getting better at existing ones)**
6. **Spirituality and emotional well-being**
7. **Contribution (giving back)**
8. **Rewards**

Press the Red Button ▶

The Wheel of Life

1. Look at the wheel of life below and, considering each area in turn, mark yourself from 1 to 10 on how happy you are with that area of your life (where 1 is 'I'm so miserable' and 10 is 'Whoopee, I'm ecstatic!'). Make a mark at the corresponding place on that feature's spoke (with 1 at the centre of the wheel, and 10 on the rim).
2. Now join the marks with a ruler. What shape is your wheel? Is it in balance? Which areas need attention? (And remember: balance doesn't mean having a 10 in all areas – although that would be

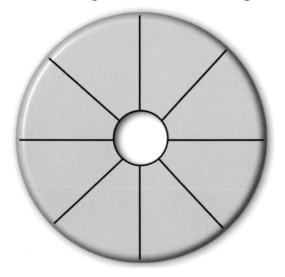

nice. At certain times in your life it will be necessary to be out of balance; for example, when you are preparing for exams. We should aim for the best balance we can achieve at any one time – so don't be too hard on yourself if your wheel looks like a squashed spider!)

3. Consider which areas you need to work on to strengthen your wheel. Plot your ideal marks on your original diagram. How does the wheel look now? Which areas have the biggest gaps between where you are now and where you want to be in the future?

4. Make a note of the areas you want to focus on most, so you can come back to them later.

Balance

We don't like to repeat ourselves, but this is important. Keeping our lives balanced is often the best way to reduce stress and anxiety.

Replay

Keeping our lives balanced is often the best way to reduce stress and anxiety.

Press Pause

Imagine you were told to get a tray with a dozen fresh eggs on it and go to the sports field. When you arrive, you're told that there's going to be a race to run the length of the football pitch with the tray full of eggs. You have to go as fast as you can, but you mustn't break any eggs.

On your marks. Get set. Go! You start to run, but the eggs start sliding

around all over the place. You stumble on a clump of grass, and two eggs smash together and start bleeding their sticky whites onto the tray. Now the surface is even more slippery. You begin to panic and decide to slow down, but the eggs still knock against each other, cracking and spitting bits of white, yolk and shell onto your shirt.

By the time you reach the goal, you are covered in more egg than Humpty Dumpty. Only two of the original twelve eggs are intact. You're tired and stressed, and maybe even a

little annoyed. Whose stupid idea was this? And who won?
The winner is smiling at you from across the pitch. They are spotlessly clean, stress-free and not even out of breath. Amazingly, their twelve eggs are still in perfect condition. The reason? The tray used by the winner was not an ordinary tray but an egg tray. The twelve eggs were balanced on the tray, allowing the winner to reach the finish line easily. 'Eggsellent,' you think to yourself. 'Look's like the yolk's on me.'

Seriously though, if the main areas of your life aren't balanced, things can get a little sticky. During out teenage years you have to spend a lot of time concentrating on our education, in particular on studying for exams. You know it's a very important and worthwhile thing to focus on, but if you spend too much time on education, your wheel may become unbalanced and cause problems. For example if you spend too much time focusing on your exams, your relationships can suffer, because you may become introverted and solitary and put no time aside for social activities and relaxing. No time for relaxing can make you stressed, and physically or emotionally unwell. Perhaps so unwell that you can't sit the exams you were preparing so hard for in the first place!

Reality Bite

People often get glandular fever as teenagers, but I didn't get it until I was thirty. It's a common but nasty virus that makes you feel tired and achy for weeks, months and sometimes years. Being ill is tough at the best of times, but a long illness like glandular fever can really take it out of you.

I felt rotten for several weeks, and found it difficult to do even simple things like make a cup of tea or watch TV. The last thing I wanted was to entertain well-meaning friends, who came to try to cheer me up.

But not seeing my friends meant that I began to get lonely. I wasn't able to work, and would worry about getting things done on time. And not going out of the house started to make me feel like a prisoner. All in all, I felt pretty miserable.

Being ill meant that all my energy was being used to fight the virus, so the other areas in my life got out of balance. When I was focused in one direction – getting better – my emotional health began to suffer. Gradually, I started to introduce more things back into my life: an afternoon with friends, or an hour of

*work. Just doing something different helped me feel a bit better.
I was soon able to do more and more, until I was fully back on
track, free of the virus and with my life in balance again.*

Xanthe is creative director for **Make it Happen**

In this book, we want to help you create and maintain a balanced life
as you begin to make things happen in your life. However, if you
experience a situation where you have your focus forced in one
particular direction (poor health or exams, maybe), try not to worry.
Simply accept that, for a time, your balance will be a little out of kilter
but that you will be able to redress this situation soon.

60 Seconds

Dream Big

1. Everyone has *permission to dream*. There is nothing to stop you
   playing a big game – in fact, we encourage it.

2. As Earl Nightingale said: *Success is the progressive realisation of a
   worthy ideal*: it is the *journey* towards achieving our dreams.

3. *Characteristics of success* include having a dream, being
   motivated, working, planning, being persistent, having good people
   skills, specializing, and being grateful.

4. Success is *personal*. Everyone has a different version of what success
   means to them.

5. Take stock with the *Wheel of Life*. Measure the most important areas
   of your life and compare them with how you would like them to be.

6. Keep your life *balanced* in order to achieve maximum success.

Up Next: What's standing in the way of your success?

▶ Now and Next 📺

NOW   Break the Barriers: What's standing in the way of your success, and what you can do about it

NEXT   The Secret to Success – and why it isn't a secret

We've looked at what success is, and how it can be achieved in very difficult circumstances. We've also looked at how keeping your life in balance can help you make things happen. But sometimes that's not enough. How many people do you know who say: 'I would like to do my homework/become a rock star/change the world, but there's no point'? When you ask them why there's no point, you'll probably get a variety of answers:

> 'Because I'm no good at it.'
> 'Because it's too difficult.'
> 'Because no one likes me.'
> 'Because it's impossible.'

You can guess what our response is. That's right:

Nothing is impossible!

All these responses are built on the person's perception of themselves and how others see them. This means they can be changed with just a little work on their belief system and their superconscious. Suddenly, anything is possible.

This episode looks at how sometimes we get in the way of our own success.

Listen Up 🎤

'**We are an impossibility in an impossible universe.**'

Ray Bradbury, science fiction author

Your Potential Power

When we embark on a long journey, most of us check that we've got everything before we set out. We make sure we've got our keys, money, bus or train ticket, sunglasses, MP3 player, and everything else we might need. However, even with this level of preparation, sometimes things slow us down: maybe our bus ticket has expired, or the train is running late. Often, these things are not our fault, and we may have little control over the situation. Or so we think.

Press Pause ⏸

You are cycling along the road on your way to somewhere really important, when you turn the corner and see a blue flashing light ahead of you. There has clearly been some sort of accident, and the traffic is beginning to build up behind it. It looks like it could be some time before the road is clear enough for you to get through. Do you:

a) **swear and shout because you want to get through?**
b) **sit down on the verge and resign yourself to waiting until the road has cleared?**
c) **get out your map to find another route to your destination?**

If you chose (c), you picked the 'empowering' belief that there was an alternative possibility to your situation. Options (a) and (b), on the other hand, both use the disempowering belief that the situation is out of your control.

Someone who can see the potential opportunities in a given situation are likely to achieve far more in their life than those who only see limiting factors. By acknowledging your potential power, there are no limits.

Reality Bite

In the 1950s, the record for running a mile was over four minutes. Anything less was regarded as humanly impossible. Yet in 1954, British athlete Roger Bannister broke the record, running a mile in 3 minutes and 59.4 seconds.

The strange thing is that by the end of 1957, 16 other athletes also broke the four-minute barrier. The current world record is 3 minutes 43 seconds – which is 16.4 seconds less than Bannister.

You see, Bannister didn't just break the record, he broke the limiting belief that the record simply could not be beaten. By breaking the record himself, he enabled others to follow in his footsteps: they realised that it was possible to run a mile in less than four minutes.

Switch On Your Potential

THE NEW
LIGHTER, BRIGHTER LIGHTBULB IS GUARANTEED TO SET YOUR ROOM ALIGHT

Simply plug into a standard ceiling connection and flick on the electric. Instantly bright. Instantly light. It's the lighter, brighter lightbulb!

We believe that potential power is a bit like a lightbulb. Let's face it, lightbulbs don't serve much purpose on their own, but when they are connected to a power source, they suddenly become very useful. With the flick of a switch, they become an instant success. We get light. Like a lightbulb, we have the potential to be more than meets the eye. Remember, we tend to use only 10 percent of our mind to power our daily activities, so there's a lot of potential still in there to make us shine more brightly. Most of us spend our days plodding along from task to task but, with the correct wiring, we could be filled with energy, determination and ability. All we have to do is spend a little time strengthening the wires of our belief system and maintaining the connection between our conscious and our superconscious. Luckily, we have plenty of ways of helping you do that.

Beware! Dreambusters

More often than not, there are people in your life who will be negative about your goals and dreams. By saying things like: 'Well, you won't be any good at . . . ' or 'You'll never be able to . . . ', they can interfere with your potential power, and even damage your route to success. We call these people dreambusters. They can pour water on your dreams, whether they mean to or not. And we all know that water and electricity don't mix!

MAKE IT HAPPEN – A Success Guide for Teenagers

Replay

Dreambusters are people who are negative about your goals and dreams. Don't listen to them!

If you're faced with dreambusters, use the techniques in this book to remain positive and committed to your goals. If you want something to happen, you're the one with the power to make it happen, whatever anyone else might say!

Reality Bite

I have never been an overly confident person, especially when it comes to school, and anything remotely academic. I have been told repeatedly by my teachers, from any early age, that exams are not my strong point. Starting my final exams was a stressful time that led me to become depressed and to have an even lower opinion of myself than before. During my first set of exams, I had a difficult time and, out of six exams, only completed one fully. Having no confidence, and that voice in my head saying 'You just can't do this. Why try?' certainly left its mark.

A friend told me about our belief systems and the power of our superconscious mind. I was amazed to find that my dreams didn't have to be out of reach! Not only that, I could find no good reason why I wouldn't be able to achieve them. Reading the life stories of other people has made me realise how much I let my fear of failing stop me from succeeding.

I am now taking my exams again (as well as sitting the ones for this year). I have six months of revision planned out and am developing my exam technique. I've also accepted that it's OK to allow people to help me. Not everything has to be a one-sided battle! I am aiming high, and applying for universities that require much higher grades than the ones I have achieved so far. There's going to be a lot of hard work, and I know that at some point I will probably want to give up, but I am determined to keep going. I believe I can do this, and I will succeed.

And if, at the end of the day, I don't get the grades I want, I know I won't be a failure. I am already a success for attempting the journey in the first place.

Hannah is studying for her final exams and looking forward to going to university to study English

Finding Evidence for Your Beliefs

Have you noticed that you can always find evidence to support your beliefs, even if they may not be true? If we believe we are weak at sport, when we score a goal or win a race, we convince ourselves that it must be a fluke. Similarly, if we're good at sport and don't score a goal or win a race, we explain this by saying that we weren't well, or were having a bad day. In neither situation are we likely to consider that we might be better or worse at sport than we at first imagined. This might not seem like a big deal, but over time a person who believes they are good at sport will find more and more evidence that this is true, and therefore, in a sense, it will *become* true. Likewise, a person who believes they are not good at sport will only find evidence to support this disempowering belief, and are unlikely to realise their potential in this area.

This can be a particular problem if your dreams and beliefs don't match. For example:

Sometimes it's not circumstances but our perceptions that get in the way of our success. This is controlled by a part of our brain called the reticular activating system (or RAS for short).

The RAS is a cluster of brain cells that controls what information we allow to filter into our brain. For example, where you are at the moment, there are probably a dozen noises nearby. There could be road noise, birdsong, shouting, or just the sound of a clock ticking or you turning the page. But you don't really hear any of these sounds, do you? If we are concentrating on something in particular, it is amazing what our RAS can filter out of our thoughts. However, if someone said your name (or even a name that sounded like yours), you would almost definitely hear them. That's because our RAS is programmed to alert us to important information that is consistent with our beliefs.

This can be very useful. We are all programmed to respond to words like 'Help!', 'Fire!' and 'Stop!'; lives are saved every day because of it. But our RAS also filters our thoughts and dismisses any information that does not support them. Because of this, our RAS won't 'listen' if we get an 'A' in English but believe we are weak in this subject. Even when we have received the good grade we can still be telling ourselves things such as 'The exam was too easy' or 'It must have been marked wrong'. Therefore is it any wonder we get caught up in this spiral of limiting beliefs?

The good news, however, is that you can deliberately programme your RAS to 'give' you the beliefs you desire. And guess what? We're going to show you how.

Reality Bite

I quite liked being grumpy. Well, that was what I told myself as I limped home every day after an eight- or ten-hour shift. I was employed as the shift manager of a local hotel and restaurant, but in reality I spent most of the day setting tables and waitressing. I would get home in a foul mood, ease my feet into a bowl of water and tuck into my first and only meal of the day, before falling into bed. No sooner had my head hit the pillow than I had to do it all again.

As the days turned into weeks, and the weeks into months, I became more and more miserable. I knew I was doing the job well, but I also knew it wasn't making me happy. Before this, I had been a teacher, had managed a busy office and had even run my own business. I was not meant to be a waitress. It wasn't fair!

The trouble was that although I believed I wasn't **meant** to be a waitress, I also believed that there was nothing I could do about it. So I would trudge to work. Limp home. Sleep. Trudge to work. Limp home. Sleep. And moan a lot. I knew I couldn't be much fun to be with, but I didn't know how else to cope with the situation. I believed I was stuck.

Finally, in desperation, my partner squared up to me and gave me an ultimatum: either do something about your job, or stop moaning. I was incensed: no one likes to be told they're behaving badly. But I hadn't appreciated the extent to which my behaviour was affecting the people I loved. Even if I was happy being miserable, they were becoming upset watching me. It wasn't an easy lesson to learn: I continued to spend a long time complaining that I had no choice and that there was nothing I could do about it. Eventually, though, something clicked in my head and I realised that I didn't have to stay in a job I didn't like. I didn't have to be miserable after all. I started looking at things more positively, and my beliefs began to alter too. Strangely, once I believed that I didn't **have** to be a waitress, doing the job seemed much more pleasant. And as well as believing that I didn't have to be a waitress, I began to believe that I could be a teacher again. And that belief made me feel good.

Less than a week after I changed my beliefs, I left my job and started working as a substitute teacher. Soon, I had an offer of a permanent job. I'm still there now, and I love every day of it. Changing my job felt like a big challenge until I changed my beliefs – then it was easy, and it was definitely worth it!

Elizabeth is now a schoolteacher and loves her job

Changing your beliefs

Before we set off to embrace our potential and fulfil our goals, it is often necessary to change some of our beliefs. Nobody can do this for you. But don't worry; we'll help out all we can.

Creating empowering beliefs

The purpose of this exercise is to replace your old disempowering belief with a new empowering one. Try to follow this exercise as closely as you can. You might prefer to ask someone to read it out to you, or you could record it and play it back to yourself so that you don't have to keep referring to the book. And remember – this really WORKS!

1. Create a relaxed state by sitting on a chair with your feet placed on the ground and your hands resting gently in your lap.

2. Close your eyes and bring into your mind a strong visual image of a new empowering belief that you wish to have in your life. For example, you may wish to be more confident.

3. Make your image bigger, brighter and stronger. As you see it more and more clearly, notice its size and characteristics. Is it in colour or black and white? Is the image still or moving? What can you hear? Smell? Taste? Feel?

4. Now imagine an image of your old disempowering belief. As you see it vividly, sense in your body the effect that it is having in your life. How does it feel?

5. Stretch your hands out in front of you, about a body width apart. Hold your palms upwards.

6. Visualise the empowering image in a sphere onto the palm of your left hand. Watch as you increase its size, making it bigger and brighter and more intense. Really feel the power of the belief.

7. Visualise the disempowering image in a sphere onto the palm of your right hand. Watch as you make it shrink, getting smaller and dimmer and less intense. Really reduce the feelings you had from this belief.

8. Now with a quick slick movement, put your left hand on top of your right hand, totally covering the tiny disempowering belief with your new enormous empowering one. Pull both your hands inwards and bang them on your chest, anchoring the positive feelings into your superconscious.

9. Repeat the process three times so that the old beliefs are completely replaced by your new beliefs and become truly eradicated from your mind.

What this exercise does is first to create a new image in your conscious mind and then anchor it into your superconscious as a belief. Like any exercise, the more you practice it, the better your results will be. Make sure you embrace, act and live your new belief and it will become a new amazing part of you. Don't forget to let us know how you get on!

Self-image

When we look in the mirror, we see an image of ourselves: a 'true' image, if you like. But we also have another view of ourselves: the one that comes from our superconscious. This image is based not just on what we see and experience, but also on our beliefs about the world, society and ourselves. Some of these beliefs may be based on fact, while others are based on the way we were brought up. These internal beliefs (our self-image) the reality and affect how we think and act. For example, or someone who appears confident may feel insecure. Fortunately, because our self-image is controlled by our superconscious, we can change our self-image, in our lives rather than a limiting one.

Reality Bite

Maxwell Maltz was a well-known plastic surgeon working in the United States in the 1960s. He performed plastic surgery on a number of women who wanted to enhance their image. On more than one occasion, however, the woman returned a year later because she thought she looked no better after the surgery. This revelation made Maxwell conclude that it was not how the woman looked that mattered, but how they felt about how they looked. This led him to come up with the following conclusion: Your self image determines our feelings, and your feelings determine your actions. Change the self image, and you can change your personality and behaviour.

Many of us believe 'false truths' about ourselves. We might think we are too fat or too short. But who makes the rules about how we should look? It's not as though there are beauty police who are about to arrest you because you don't look 'right'. Yet every year, teenagers become mentally and physically ill, and even die, as a result of problems that relate directly to their false self-image. But if we can change our beliefs from negative to positive, we can change our self-image far more easily than can be achieved through dieting or plastic surgery.

If we can change our beliefs, we can change our self-image.

'And I loved the whole idea behind the story, which is that you're beautiful, so don't let other people tell you that you're not, just because you don't look like the people in magazines. Or because you're not that weird ideal body image that's out there right now.'

Mike Myers, talking about the film *Shrek*

Self-image

Your self-image can help either bring about or prevent success. Take a few moments to think about how you view yourself. What do you like about yourself? What don't you like about yourself? Write your thoughts down and keep them in a safe place: you might want to look at them later on and see how you've changed in the meantime.

Your Notes!

The great thing about your self-image is that because it's a belief, it can be changed as easily as you changed your disempowering belief just now . You can use the same exercise as before, but this time imagine a feature of yourself that you would like to view differently. Make this feature bigger and brighter, until it replaces your old belief in your mind. Keep practicing, and you'll soon view yourself differently. Once you are your own best friend, there will be nothing to stop you making things happen.

Quiz Time!

Look at the picture below and count how many tigers there are. Don't take more than thirty seconds. When you have done that, cover the picture. Ready? No cheating. Go!

OK, now you've got the picture covered up, write down the number of lions you saw. That's right, lions.
Did you get it right?

To be fair, we were setting you up for failure in this instance. Mean, aren't we? Most people won't be able to recall how many lions are in the picture, because that's not what they asked their mind to look for. In the same way, if we sent you to the sweet shop to buy a Mars Bar, and when you came back we asked if there had been any Fruit Pastilles, it's unlikely that you would be able to remember. You were focusing on Mars Bars, so Fruit Pastilles wouldn't have been on your mind.
Our mind can only process one piece of information at a time. This might not seem a big deal: after all, it's important to have focus. But when you take a moment to think about it, what things could you be *missing* in your life because you are focusing on something else?
What things could you be missing in your life because you are focusing on something else?

If we focus on the negative, we will never see the positive. On the other hand, if we focus on the positive . . . That's right, no negatives. So it's important to remain focused on positive outcomes in order for our superconscious to remain buoyed up and eager for success. It's all down to how you react. For example, if you were awarded second place in a competition, would you be glad you'd come second, or disappointed that you hadn't come first? Your focus is everything. (We'll look at this in more detail in Episode 7.)

Press Pause ⏸

Take a few moments to think about what you could achieve by making yourself open to possibilities. Perhaps there are people who could help you make this happen whom you haven't even thought about? Or maybe, by being aware of your dreams, you may suddenly find that opportunities arise to help you fulfil them.

But remember, these are *your* dreams – not what others want for you or what you think you *should* want. External expectations only serve to increase pressure and promote confusion, so avoid them if you can.

Reality Bite

Sixteen year old Mohamed Altoumaimi followed his dream despite the odds of success seeming to be stacked against him. He pursued his lifelong interest in mathematics to crack a 300 year old formula that is normally only dealt with by much more seasoned mathematicians.

Altoumaimi's work looks at a number of complex relationships dealing with Bernoulli numbers – named after the 17th century Swiss mathematician Jacob Bernoulli - and contains complicated calculations not expected from someone who is only sixteen. In fact, when Altoumaimi approached his Swedish schoolteachers with his formula, they didn't believe it could be correct.

Not to be deterred by his teachers' unassuming expectations of him, Altoumaimi approached a professor at Uppsala University in the hope that he would be able to validate his work. Immediately, the senior maths lecturer Lars-Ake Lindahl wanted to see the work and was able to confirm not only that Altoumaimi's calculations were correct, but also that he was a very gifted mathematician.

By believing in himself and his ability, Altoumaimi was able to crack a mathematical puzzle way ahead of his years. As well as being a great achievement in itself, it has also given Altoumaimi support in continuing his dream of working in maths and physics, with the university providing additional books and tutoring to help him along.

Picture This . . .

What do you see? An American Indian face? Or an Eskimo peering into a cave? Where you direct your focus determines which image is strongest.

Awareness of Success

Listen Up

'Chance favours only the prepared mind.'

Scientist Louis Pasteur, 1854

Louis Pasteur discovered all sorts of useful things to do with diseases and vaccinations – including how to 'pasteurise' milk to get rid of bacteria. What luck, you could say. But we would say that it was no coincidence. Pasteur was unfortunate enough to have three of his five children die before they reached adulthood. This made him determined to find cures for diseases. And because that's what he was determined to do, his RAS kicked in and helped him achieve it. Brilliant.

Reality Bite

In 1960s America, racial discrimination was intense. Black people could not eat in the same restaurant as white people, and many

American states didn't allow a black person to marry a white person. If you were mixed-race, you would be shunned by both societies. Not a good start to life.

Yet one such child of the 1960s didn't allow it to define him. Being mixed race was not easy for him. Now imagine how it felt when his parents divorced and he had to live with his grandmother when his mother remarried and went to work overseas. He saw his dad only once after the divorce, and he was killed in a car crash in 1982, when he was just twenty-one.

If you'd had this sort of upbringing, how would you face the world? With resignation? Resentment? Anger? Or would you focus on something positive?

If you focus on making changes to your life and to the lives of others, you can create a vision. And that vision can be achieved, whatever your circumstances. From his school days, Barack Obama wanted to become president in order to make people happy. Instead of focusing on his background and its potential limitations, he concentrated on the future and his potential power. He believed that he could be a leader. He acted like a leader. And opportunities to follow his dream presented themselves to him. Barack Obama became the first African-American president of the United States – and, by common consent, the most powerful man in the world.

Listen Up

'**Whatever the mind can conceive and believe, the mind can achieve.**'
Success expert Napoleon Hill

Press Pause ⏸

When we look at other people's lives, we see, as long as we have a goal and a focus, you can achieve success. This applies to everyone, not just famous people with well known achievements. Take a moment to think about the role models in your life. Your parents, perhaps. Or a particular friend or relative. What have they been through to get where they are today? Think about the obstacles they might have overcome, and the commitment they have shown in order to excel in their chosen area of life. If you feel you can, why not ask them to tell you their story? You might be surprised by what you find out . . .

Reality Bite

You might think that a dyslexic teenager wouldn't have much ambition in life. With low results on IQ tests and a frustration with school rules and regulations, added to the embarrassment of being unable to read aloud in public, it would be easy to see why someone would give up on dreams of success. Luckily, Richard was not that kind of person.

Breaking away from the formality of school, Richard and his friends set up a school newspaper that brought many schools in the area together. It focused on the students not the schools and it sold advertising to major companies. When the first issue came out, Richard's headteacher wrote: "I predict you will either go to prison or become a millionaire."

The magazine continued to be a success, but when they began to sell cheap records via mail order adverts in the magazine, they stumbled onto something even bigger than the magazine subscriptions. Soon, Richard branched out to create a discount music business and 'Virgin' was born.

Since then, Richard Branson has followed his dreams of success to establish over 150 enterprises under the Virgin name. He has a personal wealth of an estimated $3 billion. He still holds the record for the fastest to cross the Atlantic Ocean by boat and he still hopes to be the first to circle the globe in a balloon.

Richard's self-belief is one of the keys to his success. His vision to succeed and his determination to follow it through is what turned an average dyslexic teenager into one of the world's most successful and respected businessmen.

So it really is possible to achieve the impossible if you have empowering beliefs, a good self-image and a strong focus. By learning how to change the things that can get in the way of your success, there should be nothing to stop you achieving your dreams. But before we get down to the nitty-gritty, let's consider what we mean by success, and whether it really is the secret people say it is.

Break the Barriers

1. *Nothing is impossible* if you are open to the idea of success.

2. We all hold *potential power*, which we can switch on to help us achieve success.

3. Don't let *dreambusters* short-circuit your potential power with their disempowering beliefs.

4. We can always find evidence for what we believe in – whether it's good or bad – because of our *reticular activating system* (RAS).

5. Our *self-image* can contain *false truths* about ourselves – but these can be changed with a simple exercise.
(Don't forget to keep practising!)

6. *Focus* helps us to be open to opportunities and possibilities.

7. *Success* can be achieved even when there appears to be insurmountable barriers in the way.

Up Next: The Secret to Success – being *success-conscious*

Episode 4:
The Secret to Success

▶ Now and Next ◻

NOW	The Secret to Success: Why it helps to be success-conscious
NEXT	Section 2: MAKE IT HAPPEN – The SUPER System of Success

Over the years, many many people have looked for the secret to success. They have tried to create a formula that anyone can use to gain untold riches and fortune. And some of these formulas work. Not surprisingly, though, it isn't always as easy as it looks: it requires action and determination. It's a pity, but you can't just read a book and wait for success to fall into your lap.

As well as knowing what success is, and how to achieve it, we have to strive for it on a daily basis. This episode looks at why it helps to be success-conscious.

Reality Bite

In America in 1908, a young journalist named Napoleon Hill was sent to interview important businessman Andrew Carnegie. Carnegie was a Scottish-born steel magnate who was in the process of giving away the great fortune he had built up.

Carnegie liked Hill and began to tell him about his idea for a 'philosophy of success' that would enable any person from any background to achieve their desires. He offered Hill the chance to spend the next twenty years finding the formula for this philosophy. Hill said 'yes' and started to interview five hundred of America's most successful men. These men had earned huge amounts of money, even though they all came from poor backgrounds and had little formal education.

(And they were all men: thankfully, anyone repeating the research today would have plenty of successful women to interview too.)

Twenty years later, Hill published his research, in the book **Law of Success**. Then, in 1929, came the Wall Street Crash and the Great Depression. In 1937, Hill turned **Law of Success** into **Think and Grow Rich**: a book that promised readers they could achieve great success if they followed the principles he set out. These principles have gone on to shape our view of success today, and we even make use of some of them in this book. In writing a book about success, Hill's greatest achievement was to inspire countless others to pursue their dreams and achieve their own success – and that includes you!

Get a Rich Life

In *Think and Grow Rich*, Napoleon Hill talks about using a secret formula to achieve financial success. However, while it's nice to have money, it's important that your life is 'rich' in other ways too.

Listen Up

Becoming rich isn't just about piling up the money. Far from it. To be successful these days, you need to be rich in happiness, friendships, health and ideas.

Sir Richard Branson

How many times have you heard people say that 'money doesn't bring happiness'? Being financially rich may make it easier for you to be happy with the life, friends, family and health you have, but it certainly won't *make* you happy. What's more, just because someone is rich doesn't mean that they know the secret of success. When the news shows famous celebrities going bankrupt, it is not because they don't have enough money, or even because they don't know how to manage their money. It's because their superconscious does not work properly for them. They are not driven by the right goals – they are money-conscious not success-conscious.

We want to show you how you can have a rich, abundant life and be successful at everything you choose to do. When you feel abundant with life's riches, just think what you can achieve – not just for you, but for all the people around you.

Poetry Corner

To Have Succeeded
by Ralph Waldo Emerson

To laugh often and love much;
To win respect of intelligent people
And the affection of children;
To earn the approbation of honest critics
And endure the betrayal of false friends;
To appreciate beauty;
To find the best in others;
To give one's self;
To leave the world a little better,
Whether by a healthy child,
A garden patch,
Or redeemed social condition;
To have played and laughed with enthusiasm
And sung with exultation;
To know even one life has breathed easier
Because you have lived . . .
This is to have succeeded.

You won't be able to stop yourself: once your mind is positively directed towards wealth, it begins to create a domino effect, producing positive changes in your life and the lives of the people around you that could never have been predicted when you began.

Hypnotist and entertainer Paul McKenna

So what, we hear you asking, is the secret to success?

Newsflash
The secret to success is the ability to manage your thoughts.

So trust us: if you can imagine something and believe in it, your superconscious helps you find the opportunities to make it happen.

Keep positive and persevere, and you *will* succeed. It's what we've been saying all along!

Replay

If you can imagine it, and believe in it, you can achieve it.

Reality Bite

Tim Berners-Lee might not be a name you recognise, but without him the world would be a very different place . . .

When he was a teenager, Tim conceived the idea of making computers connect with each other to share otherwise unconnected pieces of information. He continued to think about this throughout his physics degree and on into his work as a software designer. During his spare time, he tested his concept by building a piece of software for his own use – but that wasn't the achievement he dreamed of. As Tim says in his book **Weaving the Web**, 'the larger vision had taken firm root in my consciousness'.

Unbeknownst to Tim, several other people also had the same vision, but their ideas were never put into practice. Tim, however, knew that his idea for a 'single, global information space' was worth pursuing. He told himself that it would work. And it did. Tim invented the World Wide Web.

Tim succeeded because he believed in his idea so much that he was able to make it happen. He took the dream of a global computer network and made it a reality because he thought about it so much that his superconscious was able to find a way to make it work. In the same way, inventors throughout history have found amazing solutions to what were thought of as unsolvable problems. Imagine how life would be if someone hadn't conceived of electricity . . . or vaccines . . . or aeroplanes . . . or flushing toilets! When Einstein was asked how he came up with the theory of relativity, he said: 'By thinking about the problem intently for a long period of time.'

The trouble is that most of us give up on things too quickly. If *we think that something is impossible, or even just too much hard work, we often don't bother trying. 'What's the point?' we say. 'We're only going to fail anyway.'*

*But if we spend our time moaning about what we can't do, then we can't really blame our superconscious for giving up thinking about what we **can** do.*

Press Pause ⏸

Imagine that you are about to take a test. You've got five minutes to put together a puzzle. You've done this sort of thing before, so you're not worried. In fact, you're quite looking forward to it.

The examiner sets the timer and tells you to start. Then she walks over to your table, where the pieces of the puzzle are laid out.

'You'll never do it,' she says. 'It's impossible. No one has managed it. I don't even think it *can* be done. I'd give up now, if I were you.'

How would that make you feel? Hopeless? Annoyed? Foolish? More importantly, would you keep going?

Now imagine the examiner came over and said: 'This is really easy. You'll have it done in no time. We haven't had anyone who's found it difficult, and I'll bet you're going to be the best at it. I can see how good you are at stuff like this.'

How would you feel now? Confident? Positive? Determined? How hard would you try to complete the puzzle?

Reality Bite

Here's what Steve Jobs, CEO of Apple Computer and Pixar Animation Studios, thinks about the power of believing in success and doing what you love . . .

'I was lucky: I found what I loved to do early in life. Woz [Stephen Wozniak] and I started Apple in my parents' garage when I was twenty. We worked hard, and in ten years Apple had grown from just the two of us in a garage into a $2 billion company with over four thousand employees. We had just released our finest creation – the Macintosh – a year earlier, and I had just turned thirty. And

then I got fired. How can you get fired from a company you started? Well, as Apple grew, we hired someone who I thought was very talented to run the company with me, and for the first year or so things went well. But then our visions of the future began to diverge, and eventually we had a falling-out. When we did, our board of directors sided with him. So at thirty I was out. And very publicly out. What had been the focus of my entire adult life was gone, and it was devastating.

I really didn't know what to do for a few months. I felt I had let the previous generation of entrepreneurs down – I had dropped the baton as it was being passed to me. I met with David Packard and Bob Noyce and tried to apologise for screwing up so badly. I was a very public failure, and I even thought about running away from the Valley [Silicon Valley]. But something slowly began to dawn on me: I still loved what I did. The turn of events at Apple had not changed that one bit. I had been rejected, but I was still in love. And so I decided to start over.

I didn't see it then, but it turned out, getting fired was the best thing that ever happened to me. The heaviness of being successful was replaced by the lightness of being a beginner again, less sure about everything. It freed me to enter one of the most creative periods of my life.

During the next five years, I started a company named NeXT, another company named Pixar, and fell in love with an amazing woman who became my wife. Pixar went on to create the world's first computer-animated feature film, Toy Story, and is now the most successful animation studio in the world. In a remarkable turn of events, Apple bought NeXT, I returned to Apple, and the technology we developed at NeXT is at the heart of Apple's current renaissance. And Laurene and I have a wonderful family together.

I'm pretty sure none of this would have happened if I hadn't been fired from Apple. It was awful-tasting medicine, but I guess the patient needed it. Sometimes life hits you in the head with a brick. Don't lose faith. I'm convinced the only thing that kept me going was that I loved what I did. You've got to find what you love. This is as true for your work as it is for your lovers! Your work is going to fill a large part of your life, and the only way to be truly satisfied is to do what you believe is great work. And the only way to do great work is to love what you do. If you haven't *found it yet, keep looking. Don't settle. As with all matters of the heart, you'll know when you find it. And like any great relationship, it just gets better and better as the years roll on. So keep looking until you find it. Don't settle.'*

From http://news.stanford.edu/news/2005/june15/jobs-061505.html

Some people like the challenge of trying to prove another person wrong, but most of us achieve more when we believe we can succeed at something. No one likes to be a failure, and yet every time we tell ourselves we *can't*, or it's *impossible*, we are setting ourselves up to fail. We have made our superconscious *failure*-conscious.

In order to make things happen, we have to train ourselves to become success-conscious rather than failure-conscious. Luckily there are a few tips we want to give you to help you on your way.

So that's Section 1! You've done a great job so far: You know the foundations to achieve success. You've got your superconscious ready for action and unlimited possibilities for your dreams and desires. Most importantly, you know that you hold the key to your success in the form of your self-belief. Success is whatever your mind can create – if you can think it, you can achieve it.

Take a break and then warm up those reading muscles as you prepare to tackle the most important part of the book: learning how to Make It Happen. With our SUPER system at your fingertips, you'll be forging ahead to success in no time!

The Secret to Success

1. Success isn't achievable just by knowing the way to achieve it: you have to *strive* for it.

2. To be successful, you need to be rich in happiness, friendship, health and ideas rather than money.

3. The secret to success is your ability to manage your thoughts: if you can *imagine* it and *believe* in it, you can *achieve* it.

4. Every time we say we can't do something, or stop trying to do something, we are setting ourselves up for failure.

5. Keeping positive will make our superconscious success-conscious

Up Next: MAKE IT HAPPEN – The SUPER System of Success

Make it Happen
A Success Guide
for Teenagers

Section 1
Introduction to Success

Section 2
Making it Happen
The Super System

Section 3
Tools for Success

Episode 1
It's All in the Mind
Superconscious

Episode 2
Dream Big
Imagination

Episode 3
Break the Barriers
Empowerment

Episode 4
The Secret to
Success

Episode 5
See your
Success

Episode 6
Understand It

Episode 7
Plan Your Path

Episode 8
Execute and Reward

Episode 9
An Attitude of Gratitude
Gratitude

Episode 10
Use the Force
Affirmations

Episode 11
Heads or Tails
Positive Choice

Episode 12
Team Game
Friends

Episode 13
Manage Your
Thoughts

Episode 14
Talk the Talk, Walk the Walk
Communication

Episode 15
Never Say Never
Persistence

Over the next few episodes, we will show you just how straightforward achieving success can be. You already know the basics behind success and how your superconscious can be trained to work towards your goals, even when you're not aware of it. You also know how many successful people have used the power of their self-belief to make their dreams happen. We've taken a look at what these people *actually did* to make it happen, including our own paths to success, and we've created a SUPER System for you to put into practice in your life. Now please don't think we're bragging when we say it's a SUPER System (although of course we think it's great), it's actually a SUPER system – a handy acronym to help you get to grips with what's involved:

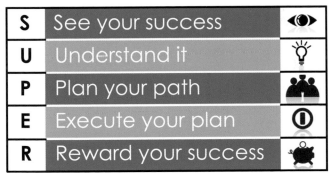

S	See your success
U	Understand it
P	Plan your path
E	Execute your plan
R	Reward your success

As we said in the Introduction, if you follow the steps laid out in this book you are *guaranteed* to succeed. There is no hidden secret to success; there is no magic formula. It is all about following some simple SUPER steps. When you're ready to find out what these steps are, then read on!

▶ Now and Next 📺

NOW ◀◉▶ See Your Success: Create a vision of
your achievement

NEXT 💡 Understand It: Find out what's driving your dreams

It's important to be clear about what you want in your life, but it's easy to become distracted and direct your attention to other things. You may feel really fired up to go for a run, for example, to fulfil your dream of becoming an athlete, but when your favourite programme comes on the television, that enthusiasm may be easily transferred to spending an hour on the sofa instead of on the track. In these instances, it's not that you don't want to achieve your dream, but rather that you don't have a clear enough *vision* in your superconscious to help you to create it. That's why the first part of our SUPER system is: See Your Success.

Channel Hop 📱

Painting Rooms

*'Today on **Painting Rooms** our designers are preparing to tackle a teenager's bedroom. So, Louis, what have you got in store for your room?'*

'Well, Sam, I'm going to be creating a luxurious den for my bedroom. Have a look at this design and you'll see what I mean. We're talking sleek lines, cool curves, silver, black, and a bit of leopard print thrown in.'

'I see. It's certainly an interesting design . . . How are you going to get the bed to hang from the ceiling like that?'

'Ah, don't you worry, Sam, I've got it all planned out. Here are my separate images, and my instructions for our carpenter to get it all together.'

'You certainly seem to have it all under control, Louis. Great job. Now, Gabby, what have you got planned for your room?'

'Well, I'm not too sure at the moment. I'm going to see where the mood takes me. It's more exciting that way, I think.'

'So, no design as yet?'

'No, but who needs a design when you have talent!'

'I see. Well, two designers, two rooms, two days, two different approaches. Time to get painting rooms!'

Two days later . . .

'Wow, Louis, your room is amazing! Just like you showed us on your design. You must be thrilled.'

'Yeah, Sam, I'm delighted. There were a few tricky moments when it looked like my plans weren't going to work, but we made some adjustments, and I'm really pleased with the result.'

'Great. And Gabby . . . um . . . well . . . it's an interesting look, isn't it? I see you've gone for lots of different colours: pink, lime, orange. What was your inspiration for that?'

'I just took it as it came, really. I liked the pink to begin with, but then I thought maybe the lime would look better. We didn't have time to get any extra paint, so I had to bring in the orange. Maybe, I should have done a design after all . . . '

'Well, it's certainly different. Let's see what our two teenage room-owners make of their new bedrooms.'

Cut to smiles of delight from Louis's room and wails of dismay from Gabby's.

Listen Up

'Fail to prepare: prepare to fail.'

Roy Keane

We can view life in a similar way to designing a bedroom: if you know what you want your life to look like, you can create a design and prepare a step-by-step plan to achieve it. If you don't know what you want, you can spend so long trying things out and changing your mind that you run out of time to do the things you wanted to do. By creating a vision of what you want your success to look like, you are taking the first step towards really making it happen. We think the best way to 'see your success' is by creating a Personal Vision Statement.

Personal Vision Statement

'Some people see things as they are and say "Why?" I dream things that never were and say "Why not?" '

Irish playwright George Bernard Shaw, 1856–1950

Most organisations have a 'vision statement' to show what they aim to do and what they value. Businesses, charities and even schools benefit from having a vision statement: it acts like a map to guide all the members of the organisation in the same direction. Because everyone knows their destination, they can all work together to reach it. Powerful stuff.

A *Personal Vision Statement* (PVS) works in much the same way, and is just as powerful. It is more than a statement of what you want in the future: it contains the guiding principles that you need to follow to get there. Most importantly, it helps you to create a powerful image of what your success will look like. Overall, a personal vision statement defines:

1. **The type of** *person* **you want to be**
   (your core values and beliefs)
2. **The type of** *life* **you want to have (your career and lifestyle)**

A personal vision statement defines the type of person you want to be, and the type of life you want to have.
For example . . .

> I am delighted to have this opportunity to work with underprivileged children in Africa. Being a care worker is a great opportunity.

> I have found my life partner and am looking forward to starting a family with them. It feels so good to have found a soulmate.

MAKE IT HAPPEN – A Success Guide for Teenagers

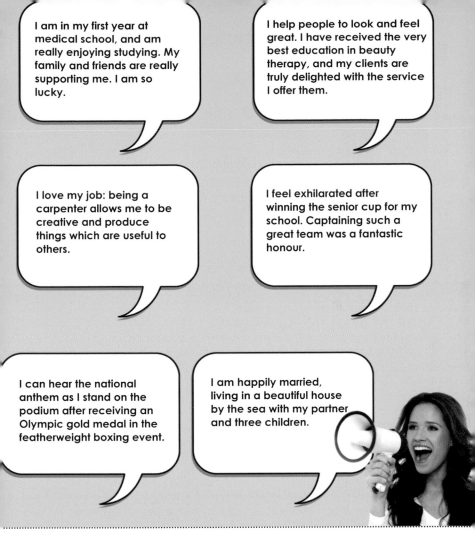

I am in my first year at medical school, and am really enjoying studying. My family and friends are really supporting me. I am so lucky.

I help people to look and feel great. I have received the very best education in beauty therapy, and my clients are truly delighted with the service I offer them.

I love my job: being a carpenter allows me to be creative and produce things which are useful to others.

I feel exhilarated after winning the senior cup for my school. Captaining such a great team was a fantastic honour.

I can hear the national anthem as I stand on the podium after receiving an Olympic gold medal in the featherweight boxing event.

I am happily married, living in a beautiful house by the sea with my partner and three children.

Some people like their PVS to contain elements for each role in their life, while others prefer to keep them simple, like the ones above. You could use the spokes on your wheel of life (see Episode 2) to help you work out which areas to focus on. The important thing is that your personal vision statement is exactly that: *personal*. It must contain *your* beliefs and opinions, not those of others, or those that others may wish you had. No dreambusters allowed!

I was raised in Kuala Lumpar, the capital of Malaysia. My mother was a strong figure in our household and had a strong vision for my three brothers and me. She had a strong belief in education: she felt that it would set us free. she communicated it to us often and with conviction, so that we believed it too.

Our family life was difficult when I was growing up. My father and mother divorced when I was eleven, which resulted in us being financially poor through my teenage years. We were all too well aware that my mother was making large personal sacrifices to give us the best education available. She expected us to give 100 percent, and we were determined to excel both for ourselves and to make her proud.

There wasn't enough money in our house to put us through college, so our only hope was to receive scholarships to get into university. My mother shared her vision of us winning the scholarships, and we knew how hard we would have to work to achieve them. Her vision became our vision. With her encouragement and support, my brothers and I each received scholarships to top universities in Malaysia.

My mother's belief in education became instilled in me and, with plenty of hard work and determination, my vision of going to university was realised. Each of my brothers also has a degree. We are all in very well paid jobs and have a standard of living which is much higher than that of our teenage years. After graduation, I came to live and work in Ireland.

During the difficult years, my mother taught me to focus on the endgame, so that I had a clear vision of my future. She always communicated the fact that our difficult upbringing was only temporary. I know that without my vision and my mother's support, my life would be very different today.

Eric is a business consultant in Dublin

'To design is to communicate clearly by whatever means you can control or master.'

New York graphic designer Milton Glaser

Writing Your Personal Vision Statement

Clear communication is essential to your PVS. So here are a few techniques to give you the best possible results:

PVS Top Tips

- *Always write in the present tense.* e.g. 'I am . . .', 'I have . . .' This will tell your superconscious that the events are actually happening, and it will learn to believe them and help you work towards them.
- *Don't worry about length.* A PVS can be ten words or ten pages long. What matters is that it holds enough information and detail for you and your future.
- *Include as much detail as possible.* When you imagine yourself achieving your vision, write down everything that is happening at that moment. This will make it more real to your superconscious. Use all five of your senses to build up a full picture in your mind: what can you see, smell, taste, touch and hear?
- *Include your feelings.* Our feelings are just as important as external sensations. Imagine how you will feel when you have achieved your vision: elated, confident, calm, and so on.
- *Use your wheel of life.* If you find it hard to come up with ideas, have another look at your wheel of life from Episode 2 to see which areas of your life could do with more focus.

Take some time to write your own PVS. Don't rush into it, but think carefully about how you would like your life to be in the future. It doesn't matter if you change your mind next week, next month or even next year: your PVS can be altered as you change. The important thing is to get started.

Listen Up

'A goal not written down is just a wish.'

Brian Mayne, author of *Goal Mapping*

Reality Bite

You're never too young to start your journey to success. This is certainly proven by the young American Cameron Johnson who started his first business, 'Cheers and Tears', aged only nine years old.

Cameron had been using his computer to make greetings cards for his parents' holiday party and soon had orders for cards from their friends and colleagues. Not long afterwards, Cameron began using the money he had earned from his greetings cards to buy Ty Beanie Babies at wholesale prices. He then sold the toys on eBay and on his Cheers and Tears website, making more than $50,000!

As a teenager, Cameron went on to start a dozen profitable businesses. By the time he was fifteen his company was making $15,000 a day in revenue and Cameron himself made his first million before he finished school.

Now in his mid-twenties, Cameron is recognised worldwide for his success as an entrepreneur and continues to branch out as an author, businessman, entrepreneur and international public speaker. His vision to create successful businesses was so clear that he was not hindered by his young age - in fact, most people who dealt with him in business had no idea how young he was. Having achieved so much already, it goes to show that there's no time like the present to get started on the road to success.

For more information about Cameron Johnson, visit
www.cameronjohnson.com

Write Your PVS!

We've already said that your PVS will be personal, but we're also aware that writing it can seem like quite a daunting task. Here are some questions that you might like to consider before you get started. It might help to create an image of yourself in your mind as you answer each question so you can really 'see' who you want to be and what you want to do with your life.

1. What sort of person would you like to be known as?
2. What inspires you?
3. What makes you happy?
4. What are you really good at?
5. What do you have strong opinions about?
6. What have you always wanted to do?
7. How/where would you like to spend your life?
8. What would you like to give back to society?

Use your answers to the questions above to write your own PVS. Then put it somewhere where you will see regularly, so that you never forget what you are aiming for.

Your Notes!

Visions Do Come True

Almost all of the true-life stories in the Reality Bite sections of this book contain examples of how people's vision to achieve success paid off. OK, so there are lots of different versions of success out there, and each of us will have a different vision of what success is. What's important is that you create your own unique vision and then make it happen!

In 2009, over three nights in a sold-out Dublin stadium, U2 performed to 250,000 people on their 360° tour. So what, you may ask: everyone knows about U2. But this wasn't always the case. Thirty-four years ago, in the same town, U2 did not exist. And now they have supporters who were not even born when their career began. Success? We think so.

In 1976, a fourteen-year-old student called Larry Mullen (U2's drummer) placed a notice on his school noticeboard to find other musicians to form a band. The initial meeting took place in Mullen's kitchen; seven teenagers showed up. One didn't return after the first practice, one left after a few weeks, and a third left a year later. By 1977, the band consisted of the four members that remain today, although at that stage they were still playing mainly cover versions of existing songs.

In March 1978, the band came first in a talent competition in Limerick: they won £500 – and studio time to record a demo. Winning the chance to make a demo helped them to get a manager and set them on the road to success. Winning also boosted the group's belief system by affirming their musical abilities. These abilities were somewhat lacking in the beginning. Bono has been quoted as saying: 'Actually, '78 was a really exciting time for U2. We had just discovered F sharp minor. So we had the fourth chord, and we'd only had three up to then.'

Today, U2 have won twenty-two Grammy awards and have sold more than 145 million albums. Recognised as the biggest band in the world, they have entertained and influenced millions of people across the generations. They have shown that their vision is more than just music but incorporates world change and motivation. This was recognised in 1999 when Kofi Annan, the

1990 UN Secretary General, paid tribute to them: 'You have made people care, and you have taught us that whether we are poor or prosperous, we have only one world to share. You have taught young people that they **do** *have the power to change the world.'*

Can't Be Bothered?

If you haven't yet taken the time to write a personal vision statement, you might want to reflect on your decision. With a PVS in place, you can see your future and what it could hold. Without one, you're just drifting about, hoping that you end up somewhere positive, but not really knowing where you're going. Living life this way is like trying to do a jigsaw puzzle without having seen the complete picture: it's still enjoyable, but it would be a lot easier if you knew what you were creating.

We all know that it's easy to read a book and not bother with the exercises, but that makes about as much sense as going to the doctor and then not taking the medicine they give you. So go on, give it a go . . . we dare you!

See your Success

1. To achieve success it's important to be able to see what it will be like.

2. Your personal vision statement is your ultimate vision of what you want to make happen in your life.

3. Write your PVS in the *present tense*, using your *senses* and *emotions*, so that your superconscious can start work on making it happen.

4. Your PVS is *personal*: don't let any dreambusters get in the way of what you really want to achieve.

Up Next: Understand It – Find out what's driving your dreams

▶ Now and Next ▢

Now Understand It: Find out what's driving your dreams

Next 👥 Plan Your Path: Planning your journey to success

When we're growing up, we learn that wanting something can be seen as rude and demanding: children who get what they want are regarded as selfish and spoilt. For the sake of politeness, the people who love us try to dampen our active 'wanting' into a more passive 'would like'. Ever been told 'I want doesn't get'?

Well, that's about to change. In order to succeed in life, and to make things happen, you *have* to *want*. Wishing for something, dreaming about something, or just thinking that you 'might like' something is not enough. And in order to really *want* your dreams to come true, you have to *understand* what it is that makes you want them: what is their purpose? Once you know the significance of what lies behind your vision of success, it's much easier to motivate yourself to go ahead and get it. Our top three motivational tips are: desire, purpose and passion.

In order to really *want* your dreams to come true, you have to *understand* what their purpose is.

🎮 Channel Hop

Successily the Teenage Witch

Successily (or Cecily, for short) was like totally 'in' with the cool crowd at school. She was the prettiest, the sportiest and the cleverest. The fact that she was also a witch was ignored due to the rest of her complete awesomeness. The problem was that the rest of the cool crowd was not so great when it came to achievement. Sure, some of them were OK on the sports field or in a maths exam, but they just seemed to lack a certain 'something'. They were full of teenage blah, meh and not-bothered. Their 'get-up-and-go' had most certainly got-up-and-gone.

Now, this didn't seem like too big a deal to the group. They were quite happy hanging out at weekends, having a laugh and fooling around. Their parents, on the other hand, were a different matter:

'Why don't you work harder?'

'What do you think your future will be like if you don't apply yourself?'

'How will you get a good job?'

'When are you going to get a haircut?'

OK, so the last question only really applied to Rufus, but his hair really **did** need a cut: everyone thought so.

The kids were sick of their parents nagging at them about the future and what they would be like when they grew up. There was no way their parents had ever been teenagers the way they were. It was impossible. Surely they'd just appeared on the planet as fully functioning, **boring** adults?

They decided to take matters into their own hands. Cecily seemed to be successful in everything she did. And she was a 'you-know-what'. Perhaps she would have the answer.

That night after school, the gang went round to Cecily's house. It didn't look haunted or anything, so they figured they'd be OK as they followed Cecily down to the cellar. There were halogen lamps dotted around, and old boxes and cobwebs. Cecily beckoned them towards a long bench, where vials of brightly coloured liquid were lined up in three rows: one of bottles containing green liquid, one of blue liquid and one of red liquid.

'You're sure you want to do this?' she asked.

The rest of the gang nodded.

'OK, well if you're sure.' She swept a glance across the

group before holding up one of the green vials. 'This is for **desire**. It will make you want your goals so badly that you can't imagine not achieving them.'

She pulled the cork out and drank

the liquid. The others took a bottle each and did the same. It tasted strange and slightly fizzy. Cecily then picked up a blue bottle.

'This will give you **purpose**. It will keep you focused on your desire until you achieve it.'

They all downed the blue liquid. Finally, Cecily picked up a red bottle.

'This is for **passion**.' One of the boys sniggered but, when Cecily glared at him, pretended to cough. 'This will keep you enthusiastic and motivated to achieve your purpose.'

The group drank the third and final potion. They looked at each other. Did they feel any different, with desire, purpose and passion swimming in their veins? They began to realise that they did. They felt empowered and excited. One by one, they left Cecily's cellar, shaking her by the hand or giving her a hug as they went.

A few moments after the last friend had left the house, Cecily's mum called down from the kitchen. 'Darling, can I have that lemonade and food colouring back now? Oh, and put your father's wallpaper table back where you found it . . . '

Whatever you want out of life, you have to understand its importance. You have to believe in it so completely that there will be no way that it *won't* happen. We call this *desire* – the feeling that you can't imagine not achieving or having what you want. The more important you understand your vision to be, the more likely it is to become a reality, because your superconscious will believe that you have already achieved it. Convince yourself of the reality of your desire, and your desire will become a reality. (And don't try knocking back lemonade and food colouring, or your teeth will go a funny colour.)

Replay

Convince yourself of the reality of your desire, and your desire will become a reality.

 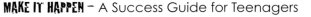

I've always loved ideas, the more creative or unexpected the better. Some people change channels or fast-forward when it comes to commercial breaks, but I know that the advertising is often the best thing on television. It certainly costs more per second to make than the average programme.

I can remember jingles better than I remember some songs. I can gaze at a poster for ages, enjoying the concept and art direction. So when I discovered that people actually work in an industry that creates advertising, I wanted to join. I mean, I **really** wanted to join. It wasn't for the money; it was because of my passion to inspire and communicate.

I knew it was going to be tough. Everything I read about the advertising industry told me how competitive it was, how it was dominated by the brightest people, who had been to the best universities. I didn't consider myself close to that, but I believed that I could still work in the industry. I just needed a plan to get a foot in the door. By keeping an open mind, I mapped out all the possible routes into the industry and created a six-step strategy. I was willing to work as a receptionist first (step five), if I had to. I was **going** to work in advertising. Nothing else mattered.

I read trade journals, websites and books. I spoke to everyone I could find who worked in advertising about what they thought of the industry and how they got their first break. I started recording the ad breaks. I even bought newspapers and magazines just to pull out the ads, so I could stick them on my wall and study them. I made it the most important goal in my life at the time: when I wasn't studying, I was absorbing as much as I could about marketing and communication.

There are two sides to advertising – client management and creative services – and I soon learnt that I had to choose one or the other. Because it was the more open route at the time, I chose client management (even though I'm a creative at heart). I started applying to every graduate-recruitment programme I could find.

Advertising agencies tend to have strange questions on the application forms, so I had to take risks and push my responses to the next level. I rejected my first, second and third ideas, and kept pushing until I'd come up with answers that had energy and demonstrated my passion. I knew that I had to stand out – just like the best advertisements – and for all the right reasons.

I kept every rejection in a file: they were a record of what I had done. Each of them was, in its own way, an achievement. Who cared if they'd said no: I had taken action. I reminded myself about my friends who hadn't even applied for the jobs they wanted. I had, at least, tried.

To tell the truth, I did get down after receiving some of the rejections. But when this happened, I looked up at my wall, with its great examples of advertising, and it inspired me to keep going. This was the reason I wanted to be in the industry: to work with powerful ideas and great images.

Then I got through to first-round interviews with two top agencies in London. After two more rounds of interviews at one agency, I was offered a job. Just me and one other graduate, for an agency that had received over a thousand applications! I'd made it at last. I had become an account manager in advertising – but that was just the beginning of my plan. After a couple years, I made the jump to the creative side, and became a copywriter. And I still think the ads are the best thing on the box!

Benjamin is a writer and model and lives in Norwich.

Dreaming

Dreaming is essential when it comes to building desire because it helps you to understand the importance of your personal vision by actively experiencing it in your imagination. But before you rush off to bed or collapse on the sofa for a nap, perhaps we should make clear the difference between dreaming when you are asleep and daydreaming. Ordinary dreaming is part of your REM sleep – where, it is believed, your brain processes all the stuff it has learnt during the day. REM sleep can even help you learn because, while you are asleep, you repeat things you have done consciously while you are unconscious. So, when you come to do them again, your superconscious knows exactly what to do. Maybe you should go and have that nap after all .

Daydreaming, on the other hand, is something we do while we are awake. Unfortunately, daydreamers can get some bad press: they are seen as lazy, and oblivious to real life. But don't be fooled by the stereotype: there's a vast difference between people who dream to avoid the things in life they don't like (studying, perhaps, or visiting relatives) and those who dream to create the things in life they *do* like.

Dreamers v. Achievers

The difference between dreamers and achievers is the transition from the dream to the *desire*. Stereotypical daydreamers drift off into their own thoughts and wonder about how nice it would be to be at home in bed, or out with their mates, or eating a burger. Achievers, however, dream about things they want to *do* in life; things they want to *achieve*. And the more they think about what they want, the more they feel the need, or the *desire*, to do it. It's like building a bonfire: you start out with a couple of twigs and a match to make a flame, but as the twigs catch light, the flames get bigger. Add more wood, and the flames get bigger still. In the same way, if you want to achieve something, keep dreaming the dream, until the desire gets so big that it would be unthinkable for you *not* to achieve it.

Reality Bite

We think Susan Boyle is a real hero. What a talented but humble woman!

While her talent is admirable, it is her story which is extraordinary: her courage, her determination, and her passion to follow her dream.

Susan was diagnosed with learning difficulties at school, and got the nickname 'Susie Simple' when she was bullied by the other children. After leaving school without qualifications, she was employed on a government training programme for six months, as a trainee cook. This was to be the only time in her life she was employed.

From the age of twelve, Susan loved to sing; her main experience of singing was in the local church. She spent most of her adult years caring from her mum; even though her dream was slipping away with the years, she always put her mother first.

In 1999, she recorded a charity album featuring the song 'Cry Me a River'. In the same year, she spent all her savings on a professionally cut demo, which she sent to record companies, talent competitions, and local and national TV stations. Sadly, Susan was ridiculed in competition and almost abandoned her plan to audition for the **Britain's Got Talent** television show because she felt that she was too old.

Fortunately, Susan's passion won out: her audition for **Britain's Got Talent** was the first time she had sung in public since her mother died. When she went on stage, on 11 April 2009, and sang 'I Dreamed a Dream' from the musical **Les Misérables**, Susan's life changed. Her dream had come true, at the age of forty-nine.

Millions of people were touched by her performance. The contrast between Susan's plain appearance and her incredible singing voice stunned those who had dismissed her at first. Susan is now famous worldwide. Her story is truly inspirational: she has encouraged others to grasp their dreams and never give up.

Press Pause ⏸

- Take a minute or two to think about something you want to achieve in life. Make a note of it.
- Ask yourself: how badly do I want it? Write down a number from 1 to 10 (where 1 is 'Not really bothered' and 10 is 'So badly I could scream').
- Now, think about it again. Like the exercises you have done already, imagine yourself actually being there, doing what you set

out to achieve. What can you see, hear and smell? What are people saying to you? How are you being congratulated on your achievements? Make all the senses louder and brighter. Really *live* the success.

- Now ask yourself again: how much do I want it? Make a note of your score, between 1 and 10.

Has your score increased? If you have put the time and effort into dreaming about your goal, your desire to achieve it should have got bigger. The more you repeat this exercise, the more desire you will have to be the success you have always planned to be.

Press the Red Button ▶

Understanding Your Vision

Step 1 in the SUPER system was to "See" your success. Hopefully you have completed the exercise in the last chapter and have written your PVS (Personal Vision Statement) - If you haven't then do it now. Have faith; it is really important to write these things down.

The next step is to understand the reasons why you want to achieve that vision. Once you have a strong enough reason then you can do anything. Take some time now and write all the reasons why you want to achieve that vision of your future. Do you want to fulfil all your talents? We all want to maximise our own capabilities. Do you want to feel happy with who you are? How would the achievement of the vision help you to accomplish that? Do you want to be able to do the things you want in life? Do you want to have more time to spend with your friends, doing the things you really enjoy? Do you want to make your parents proud? They have done a lot for you, what can you do for them? Do you want to help people less fortunate? Do you want to make a difference? Whatever the reasons, take some time now and write them down.

Your Notes!

In Episode 2 we talked about motivation and how it is important for success. Writing down the reasons why you want to achieve something can be really motivating. It helps you to understand why you want to achieve success.

Here's an example that will help you:

Imagine you're standing on top of a 50 storey building. As you look down over the edge, all you see are little dots, like ants, moving around on the ground. Now imagine there is a 3 inch wide beam connecting your building to another. Would you walk across that beam? If the beam was laid on the ground you could easily do it. But when it's 50 storeys up it's a different scenario. How motivated on a scale of 1 to 10 are you to walk across that beam? (Circle your answer below)

1   2   3   4   5   6   7   8   9   10

Most people aren't very motivated. Some would even say zero on a scale on 1 to 10. But imagine now that the building you are on is on fire. Now on a scale of 1 to 10, how motivated are you to walk across that beam? (Circle your answer below)

1   2   3   4   5   6   7   8   9   10

For most people their motivation will have increased, but for some they will still be very reluctant. They may have a fear of heights and would ask many more questions before they would walk across. How big is the fire? Is there a fire escape? Could the fire be put out? Can I be rescued in some other way? They are all valid questions.

But think of a third scenario, same buildings, same beam, but this time someone you love is trapped and their life depends on you getting across that beam. On a scale of 1 to 10, how motivated are you now, to walk across that beam? (Circle your answer below)

1   2   3   4   5   6   7   8   9   10

In this case most people would circle 10. Compare this to the first question, where the typical answer is 1 or 2. Ask yourself what was different about the process in the three scenarios - not the mental aspects of the process, but the physical ones. The answer of course, is there was nothing different. It was the same building and the same beam. The motivation was highest in the third scenario because of your reason why. Because you had a strong enough reason, you were able to overcome your fears or any other obstacles that lay in front of you.

This is the power behind *understanding* the reason why you want to achieve your vision. If you haven't already done so then go back to the Red Button Exercise and complete it. Make sure you have a strong reason why in there, in order to ensure you will succeed.

Failure: It's Not All Bad!

Of course, we're not saying that achieving your dreams is going to be easy. There aren't many people in the world who have achieved their goals without coming up against obstacles. But remember, failure isn't a destination: it is a temporary diversion on your journey to success.

Reality Bite

From an early age, J. K. Rowling had an ambition to be a writer. She often tried her hand at writing, but little came from her early efforts.

However, in 1990, on a train journey from London to Manchester, she had the idea for the Harry Potter series. The ideas excited her, and she became very enthusiastic as she planned the story in her head. The train was delayed for over four hours, but because she didn't have a pen, and was too shy to ask anybody for one, she didn't write down any of her ideas. When she arrived in Manchester, she began work on the book immediately, although it would take her several years to complete it.

By 1994, Rowling was still trying to finish her first book. She was also working full time, and bringing up her daughter as a single parent. Eventually, she finished her first copy, and sent it off to various agents. After she had found an agent, it took more than a year for the book to be taken on by a publisher: the publisher paid her an advance of £1,500 and advised her to keep working, because writers of children's books don't tend to be very well paid. The initial print run for **Harry Potter and the Philosopher's Stone** was just a thousand copies.

The rest, as the say, is history. Within a few weeks of the books publication in 1996, sales started to take off. Rowling received a grant to allow her to write full time. After the book's initial success in the UK, Scholastic paid a remarkable £100,000 for the rights to publish the books in America. In 1998, Warner Bros secured the film rights for the books, and today Harry Potter is one of the most widely recognised media products in the world.

Yet Rowling could have given up at many points along the way: when she had no pen; when she had to work to earn money; when she had to raise a child on her own; when she couldn't get an agent; when she couldn't get a publisher. It must have often seemed to her that she was going to fail. Thankfully, Rowling saw these setbacks as obstacles to overcome. And overcome them she did – to the great benefit of both herself and Harry Potter fans.

The point is that even if you're failing at something, you are still on the way to achieving it. So it is important to keep going, even if it looks like you're heading in the wrong direction. By understanding what impact achieving your success will have on both you and others will keep you focused on the vision you wish to achieve. Eventually, your work will pay off, and you will reach a turning point that will take you to a successful conclusion.

Even if you are failing at something, you are still on the way to achieving your goal.

But remember: if you give up, there's no chance that you will get where you want to go. You'll still be right where you started.

Keeping Passion Alight

When people talk about passion, they often say it's like fire. It can be ignited; it burns; and it is even said to be 'white hot'.

When we talk about being passionate about achieving our goals, we mean all these things. Our desire should make us so excited about the outcome that we feel as if we are full of fire: it shows us why we really *need* to make our dreams a reality. And when we have that fire inside us, we find it much easier to follow the more active, practical steps that will lead to us achieving success.

Reality Bite

Raynece Leader-Thompson was thirteen when she created the Math-a-Mania game, which soon became so popular in her home town of Tulsa, Oklahoma that she and her mother began travelling across the United States to promote the game to both students and teachers.

Raynece's vision may have been to create a game, but her inspiration and purpose for the vision was to make learning maths fun. She understood the importance her dream had and used it to keep her motivated towards its success. Once the game was developed and marketed, Raynece became aware of another issue she wanted to address. Having visited many schools across the country, she began to see how few resources teachers had in the classroom. With her desire to help others as the understanding behind her goal, Raynece set up at 'Teacher's Wish List' on her website. A percentage of the game's sales are set aside to grant teachers' wishes for their classrooms, which the teachers request via a form on the website. Every three months an independent panel decides who should receive the prize and the supplies are sent to the school.

Through her understanding and purpose of making a difference in learning mathematics, Raynece has been able to create a successful business that gives something back to students and teachers across the United States. As her passion continues, so will her success.

For more about Raynece, visit www.mathworkz.com

Cooking with Chef Desiree

'Today we join Chef Desiree as she makes her famous passion cake. So, Desiree, what's the secret to your passion cake?'

'Well, Michael, if I told you that, I'd have to kill you! Ha ha ha ha!'

'Ha ha. Yes. Of course. So, tell us what you're doing . . . '

'Absolutely. First of all, we take a large bowl. The larger the bowl, the larger the cake. And I like it large, don't you, Michael? Ha ha ha . . . Next, we need our first ingredient. Now, many people use flour, but I'm not like other people, no sir. Instead of flour, I use hope.'

'Soap? But isn't that a bit, well, soapy?'

'No, Michael, not soap. **Hope!**'

'Hope?'

'That's right. It's amazing how a bit of hope can add substance to a cake. Of course, you can find hope in various forms, but I prefer organic hope, straight from the superconscious – and before you ask, no, that's not the new supermarket off the bypass.

'So, we take the hope and combine it with an equal helping of faith. Now, faith can be bought loose or in packets, but you're going to need a fair bit, so don't skimp! Make sure you don't put in too much though, or you'll be faith-full. Get it? Faithful! Ha ha ha ha ha . . .

'Right. After the two ingredients are mixed together, we can add in some courage. Those of you who like their cakes to have a little 'kick' can add Dutch courage, but mostly the good old traditional non-alcoholic courage will be fine. Ha ha ha . . .

'Finally, we combine all the ingredients with a splash of tolerance. Semi-skimmed is great, but you do need plenty to really help the passion cake rise. And that's it. Put it in the oven at 180 degrees for forty minutes, and your passion cake should be crisp and golden. Delicious!'

'That's fantastic, Desiree, thank you. So, just to recap, for the perfect passion cake, you'll need: **hope, faith, courage** and **tolerance**. Next on the cooking channel . . . how to make Dream Topping.'

The problem with fire is that, without enough fuel, it can easily go out. And just like being cold makes it harder to work, so not having the heat of fire within you makes it harder to follow the other steps to your goal. It may sound unimportant compared to the other steps in the SUPER system, but if you don't understand and truly believe in the significance of your success and what a great impact it will have both in your life and the lives of others, it's all too easy to lose motivation and even give up on your dreams completely. Remember, it takes U to be SUPER!

60 Seconds

Understand It

1. In order to really *want* your dreams to come true, you have to *understand* what their purpose is.

2. *Desire* makes you want to achieve your goals so badly that you won't be able to imagine not achieving them.

3. *Passion* will keeps you enthusiastic and motivated to achieve your purpose.

4. *Dreamers* can be *achievers*: take time out to visualise your achievements.

5. *Failure* is a part of success. If you don't try, and try again, you will never succeed.

6. Use *hope, faith, courage* and *tolerance* to help keep your passion and understanding alive.

7. It takes U to be SUPER.

Up Next: Plan Your Path to success with SUPER goals

Episode 7:
Plan Your Path

Now and Next

NOW Plan Your Path: How creating and using SUPER goals can help you succeed, step by step

NEXT Execute and Reward: How to work through your goals and feel great about it.

Once you have written your personal vision statement and you understand why your vision is important, it may seem like a daunting task to make it happen. Where do you start?

Pop Quiz
Q. How do you eat an elephant?
A. One bite at a time.

When a task seems overwhelming, the best thing to do is to break it down into smaller parts. That way, you only have to focus on one thing at a time. If you *did* want to eat an elephant, eating one a bite at a time would be far more manageable than trying to eat it all at once.

Listen Up

'The secret to getting ahead is getting started. The secret to getting started is breaking your complex, overwhelming tasks into small, manageable tasks, and then starting on the first one.'

Mark Twain, American author and humourist

Press Pause

You order a new desk from a mail-order company, but when it arrives, the package looks suspiciously flat. You tear open the cardboard and what looks like a million pieces fall out all over the floor. Nightmare! Where will you start?
Do you:

a) just get stuck in? You have a pretty good idea of how it should be put together.
b) look at the picture on the box and try to work out how to build it using that?
c) find the instructions and follow each step until you've created the finished product?

Most of us wouldn't begin to do something complicated if we didn't have instructions to follow. Instructions break things down into simple steps, enabling us to achieve more than we would be able to do without them. Some people say that they wish their life came with a set of instructions. Unfortunately, we don't have this luxury. However, it is possible to create a set of *goals* to use as a plan to help you achieve your dreams.

Channel Hop

Secret Agent Happen

Agent Happen tore along the dirt track. The dust kicking up around his feet made his target harder to see, as the distance between them increased. How the evil villain Dr Buster had managed to steal that girl's bicycle was something Happen would never comprehend. Perhaps if he hadn't stopped to buy the kid a lollipop, Happen would have Buster in his reach right now. The thought made his top lip twitch with anger. He cursed the spy division for not putting rocket wheels in his shoes, like he'd asked.

Ahead of him, the pink and silver bicycle cornered sharply, the sparkling streamers flying out behind Buster's ungainly frame as he pedalled frantically. By the time Happen rounded the corner, only seconds later, the bike was in a heap on the floor, and Buster was gone.

The sound of an engine roaring into life made Happen turn round. Speeding out from behind the jetty was Buster's speedboat, **Dreambreaker**, with Buster at the helm.
'So long, Happen!' Buster called into the wind. 'You won't catch me this time!'

As the waves from the boat slapped against the shore, Happen looked around him in despair. There were no other boats in sight, and Buster was already making headway across the lake, slaloming between the rocks.

The rocks! That was it! Happen peered across to the other side of the lake. It was a long way, and there was no guarantee that he'd find Buster when he reached the other side, but he had to try. He steadied himself on the jetty and prepared to jump to the first rock, scrambling onto the outcrop as he landed. From here, he looked around him once again. The next rock was easily within reach. He jumped again, and pulled himself up, hardly even getting his suit wet.

Happen made his way like this across the lake, one rock at a time. He had almost made it to the other side when a plume of smoke caught his attention. Buster's boat was smashed against the jagged rocks, and a dark cloud of smoke was hanging over it. Happen crouched down and shielded himself from the blast, as bits of boat rained down around him. The boat's name splashed into the water: **Dreambreaker** was now only driftwood.

Happen smiled to himself. 'Sometimes it pays to plan where you're going,' he said in an imaginary voiceover. 'Dr Buster is now nothing but fish food.'

With that, he jumped to the shore and sprinted off towards the horizon.

We can use goals like stepping stones to help us reach our ultimate dream and make it a reality. Like Agent Happen jumping from rock to rock, if we focus on the two or three goals closest to us, we can accomplish these, and then move on to the next set of goals. Before we know it, we're right where we want to be: making things happen!

Reality Bite

Some people appear to be naturally funny and quick-witted, no matter what the situation. Having a spontaneous, humorous response to everything is something which never came naturally to me. However, I always believed that it was a great ability – and one which I would love to possess. But could I learn it? I decided to take on a challenge: to do a stand-up comedy course. At the end of the course, I would do a stand-up routine in front of a real live audience.

Stand-up comedy is incredibly difficult: an audience's response to weak humour is immediate and, at times, cruel. However, for those who succeed, their ability to respond to their audience and engage in humorous interaction is a delight to see.

So, I enrolled on the course. Some of the other people on it wanted to become professional comedians, while others, like me, wanted to improve their communication style. My concern was: could comedy be taught? Or was I wasting my time? Our instructor, Aidan Killian, dismissed the idea that comedy is a natural ability. He told us that the best comedy is the most frequently rehearsed and the most thoroughly prepared. In fact, he said that he performed his act two hundred times in front of family and friends before using the routine in public. So, 'spontaneous comedy' was not spontaneous at all! This was comforting: maybe I wasn't wasting my time after all!

Then Aidan started breaking it down. He spoke about the 'formula' for comedy: timing, planning, the punchline, and the different ways to lead in to a punchline. It had never occurred to me before that comedy could be broken down like this.

We worked on our sets and met Aidan a few times to perfect our acts. He constantly reminded us that success comes with practice; there are no born comedians. He spends hours every day developing jokes and trying to craft humour from particular events.

In the days leading up to the night, I visualised myself performing superbly, the crowd laughing, and me getting a massive round of applause at the end of the set. The night came, and I was very nervous. Could I pull it off? The house was full. I was the third act on stage. The first act was a regular on the comedy scene. He was very good, and everybody was laughing and having a great time. How do I follow this, I wondered. Could I find a way out of going on stage?

Then, I suddenly decided not to give any room to these thoughts. I focused on my breathing, developed my composure, and once more ran through the successful delivery of my set in my head. And then I heard: 'And now, give a big round of applause to Philip O'Callaghan!' I stood up and ran on to the stage, telling myself to relax and enjoy it. I began my set, and the audience responded with laughter: most of the punchlines worked! When I'd finished, I got a big round of applause, just as I'd visualised.

I had successfully completed three minutes of stand-up comedy and, more importantly, I now had the confidence to feel that I could do it again. The professionals may not be quaking in their boots, but I know that comedy, like any other skill, takes planning, practice, patience and persistence. It was all about breaking the process down into manageable pieces. Now I had the confidence, and if I added to that the drive, motivation and desire, I felt I could take things to the next level.

It's the same with anything: when you break it down into smaller components, they become manageable. The three-minute, stand-up routine becomes a story with nine punchlines. Three punchlines, and you're a third of the way there. And once you start, there's no stopping you.

*Philip is a director of **The Super Generation** and co-author of* ***Make It Happen***

Goals

Once we've got our vision, we need to make it more attainable by turning it into a goal. Goals are simple, direct requests that we can make happen. To make a vision into a goal, we need to toughen it up a little. (We also need to be able to carry it out and execute it, but more on that in the next episode.) For example:

Vision	Goal
I'd like to be a world-class musician.	It is now December 2012, and I am a member of a band.
I wish I had more friends.	It is now July 2013, and I have made ten new friends.
I wish I didn't have spots.	It is now September 2012, and I have spot-free skin.

The goals will help us to achieve our personal vision because they contain focused projects for us to work with. Once we start work on our goals, our personal vision will soon be within reach. Remember:

If it is to be, it is up to me!

You can see from the table that, like a PVS, goals are written in the present tense, with a positive focus. It is also important that they contain a time element to remind you when to work on them, and to help you see when they have been achieved. We've already used the *SUPER* mnemonic to explain our system of success, but we can also use the word SUPER here to help us construct our goals:

Channel Hop

Supergoal!

Is it a bird? Is it a plane? No, it's *SUPERgoal!*
More powerful than a dream, more effective than a wish, more gutsy than your average goal, *SUPERgoal* creates the ultimate in achievable goal-setting. In an ideal world, every goal should be *super*:

S	*Specific*, in terms of outcome and timeframe (e.g. It is now [future date] and I have/am _____)
U	*Up* to you (Something you can achieve, not someone else's responsibility)
P	*Positive* and *present tense* (Lets your superconscious start work straight away)
E	*Environmental* (Good for others around you, as well as the natural world)
R	*Recordable* results (Some way of testing or measuring whether you have achieved your goal)

Press the Red Button ▶

Constructing Your Goals

There are lots of different ways to construct goals for your PVS. To start you off, we'll use a process inspired by master goal-writer Brian Tracy. The time limits in each section are important because they force your superconscious to come up with 'real' answers that you might not think about if you take longer and let your conscious mind get in on the act. So find a clock or stopwatch, and have a go at the steps below.

1. Take thirty seconds to write down the three most important things that you want to achieve in the next year.
2. Using the eight success areas from Episode 2: Dream Big (health, relationships, money, career, education, spirituality, contribution and rewards), write down the three most important things that you want to achieve in each area in the next year. Take thirty seconds for each area.
3. You should now have a list of twenty-four goals for the next twelve months. Don't panic, we're not going to ask you to do all of them! Instead, highlight the five or so goals that stand out the most to you.
4. Take a little time to rewrite these goals using the SUPER mnemonic to make them more focused. All your goals should be in the following format: It is now [future date] and I am/have . . . ' When you're happy with your goals, copy them onto small pieces of card and decorate them with colours and images to make them more memorable (to you and your superconscious).

Your Notes!

Fraser Doherty has taken the word 'super' to an even greater level, using it as the name of his own brand of preserves: Super Jam. When he was eleven, the young lad from Edinburgh made his first attempt as an entrepreneur by hatching a couple of eggs and then rearing the chicks so that he could sell their eggs to make a profit. Sadly, this plan came to an abrupt end when a fox got into the garden and killed the chickens. ☹

Fraser wasn't one to give up on a dream of success and when he was fourteen he and his gran spent an afternoon together making her secret recipe jam. He soon found that the jam's fabulous, healthy, sugar free recipe was temptation enough to get his neighbours to buy the product.

Without a vision, most people would have stopped there: a few jars of jam to a few friendly neighbours. Not Fraser. He made more jam which he sold to more neighbours and then at the local church fete. Soon he was producing a thousand jars of jam a week from his mum and dad's kitchen.

Again, most people would have stopped there. Fraser, however, had a plan of action and did a deal with a factory in the north of England to make and distribute his product. Once he achieved his qualifications to get into university, Fraser took time out to concentrate on the business. Soon he had deals with major UK supermarkets and by 2010 there were 500,000 jars of Super Jam being produced each year.

Fraser's vision knows no limits. Still not in his twenties, he has moved on to talks with a chain of major health food superstores in America and it seems like his business, and his success, will keep on growing.

Programme Your Superconscious for Success

In the same way that we have to set our television to record particular programmes, we have to set our superconscious to record our goals. By recording our goals a number of times, we can make sure they are stored in the belief system of our superconscious mind. We already know once we believe something, we act on it automatically, and with better results.

Recording Your Goals

1. Order your goal cards by the date you have set to achieve each goal. It's important not to become overwhelmed by what lies ahead of you, so pick out the two or three that are most important right now.

2. Each morning when you wake up, grab these goal cards and read your goals, three times. Use all your senses to help you see, hear, feel, taste and smell (yes, really) each goal, as though it is actually happening as you say it.

3. At the end of the day, before you go to sleep, do the same thing again. You already know this, but the repetition will help your superconscious believe in your goals, and you will open yourself up to the amazing people who can help you achieve them.

Imagining our goals actually happening is a technique that many top sports people (and others) use.

Reality Bite !

At only twenty-six, Denis O'Regan is one of Ireland's best known young jockeys, having won the Galway Plate, the Irish Grand National and many overseas events.

Horses were Denis's first love. From a very young age, he loved everything about them, and spent weekend after weekend and summer after summer with them. Indeed, they seemed to be his sole passion.

Of course, many young people are interested in horses. But Denis was different. He wanted to be a champion jockey, like his cousin, who had won the Irish Grand National two decades earlier. Denis was certainly very good with horses, maybe not significantly better than other young people. However, his attitude was completely different.

He knew what he wanted, and used every moment he had

to perfect his riding ability.

Early on in secondary school, he got a summer job as a stable boy with one of the best trainers in the country. Denis saw the job not as a chore but as a great opportunity to learn from the best. During the outbreak of foot and mouth disease in 2001, horses were not allowed to be taken out riding, and racing was temporarily suspended. During this period, Denis trained on a dummy horse for many hours each day. And his passion, perseverance and self-belief paid off. Denis built on his strengths, worked hard, and eventually achieved his dream.

In 2005, Denis won the Galway Plate. Before the race, he had spent time preparing mentally as well as physically. His trainer, Dermot Weld, gave Denis a video showing the previous year's winner, David Casey, as he completed the race: Denis watched the tape again and again.

Then, just before the big day, Weld walked Denis round the course. The young jockey imagined himself and his horse, Anser, crossing the finishing line ahead of the other competitors. The visualisation paid off: on the day of the race, he and Anser came home as winners .

Denis claims that winning the Galway Plate kick-started his riding career. In fact, his success was down to the fact that he had single-handedly pursued his passion for horses.

Denis used the techniques we have shown you to programme his superconscious to believe that he would be a champion jockey, well over a decade before he became one. And in the case of the Galway Plate, he had programmed his superconscious mind to win before he even started the race.

Listen Up

'**Always bear in mind that your own resolution to succeed is more important than any one thing.**'

Abraham Lincoln

We know that you have the power to make things happen and to be a success. Now you have a plan to help you get there. By committing yourself to your goals and reminding your superconscious to help you create them, you are already on that journey to success. Now it's time to really get started!

Plan Your Path

1. Goals act as stepping stones towards your personal vision statement.

2. Goals are more focused than dreams: they are simple, direct requests that we can make happen.

3. Goals should be *SUPER*: **S**pecific, **U**p to you, **P**ositive, **E**nvironmental, and **R**ecordable.

4. Focus on the two or three most important goals at a time.

5. Use your goals cards first thing in the morning and last thing in the evening to remind your superconscious what it needs to be working on.

Up Next: Execute and Reward – How to work through your goals and feel great about it.

Episode 8:
Execute and Reward

▶ Now and Next 📺

NOW ① Execute and Reward: How to work through your goals and feel great about it.

NEXT   SECTION 3: Tools for Success

We've covered the first three steps you need to take to achieve success:

S	See your Success
U	Understand It
P	Plan your Path

Now it's time to get stuck in and look at the remaining two parts of our SUPER system for success:

E	Execute
R	Reward

Let's take a look first at how best to execute our plans and take action to achieve our goals.

Listen Up

'The will is to select a goal, determine a course of action that will bring one to that goal, and then hold to that action till the goal is reached. The key is action.'

Michael Hanson

Actions Speak Louder than Words

Without action, not a lot gets done. Imagine a film set with all its lights and cameras waiting to roll. The actors are getting into position, and the director is checking his script. Everything is ready to go. The clapper-loader names the take, and the director calls out: 'Lights . . . Camera . . . ' And then he stops. What happens? Nothing. No action.

The actors are just standing there under enormous lights like in some giant freeze-frame photo. Not very interesting – and certainly not worth watching at the cinema. But if the director shouts 'Lights . . . Camera . . . Action!' suddenly the set spins into activity. The actors move and deliver their lines, special effects go off, and the set becomes a very exciting place to be.

In the same way, we can have our personal vision statement and goal cards always to hand, but unless we motivate ourselves to execute them, they will remain just words on a piece of paper. It's only once we shout 'Action!' and start moving towards our goals that things become exciting.

Press Pause ⏸

Think of a time when you achieved something that you were really proud of. It might be a sporting achievement or a piece of school work, perhaps. Remember how good the feeling of success was.

Now slowly rewind your memory and examine the events that led up to your achievement. What did they involve? What did you have to do to reach your goal?

Now think about what would have happened if you hadn't put your efforts into the task. Would you have achieved the same level of success? The great thing about action is that once you start, it's usually very easy to keep going.

Reality Bite

La Tonya King is a sixteen-year-old boxing champion from Detroit in the United States. She already holds six national titles and one world title, taking on opponents who are often 25 pounds heavier than she is. However, not only is La Tonya a success in the ring, she has also continued her studies to maintain her good grades in school

Looking back, the inspiration for La Tonya's success was when she was eleven and saw her younger brother getting beaten up by some older boys. La Tonya's protective instinct kicked in and she immediately took action to protect her brother by fighting off the boys herself. When her parents sent her brother for boxing lessons to learn to defend himself, La Tonya decided to join in too.

Once she started training, she set her sights on success: her vision is to get a college scholarship and to meet her idol, Oprah Winfrey. In order to achieve this, she needs to excel at both boxing and academia, picking up successes along the way by winning fights and getting A grades in school. And the only way she can do that is to keep going: keep training and keep studying. As La Tonya says herself: 'It all comes from discipline. I am really focused on what I am doing.'

 **Tech Specs**

Physics Fun

Sir Isaac Newton (he of discovering-gravity fame) used his enormous brain to work out what are now known as the Three Laws of Motion. According to his first law: '*An object at rest* remains at rest unless acted on by an unbalanced force. *An object in motion* continues in motion with the same speed and in the same direction unless acted on by an unbalanced force.'

We know this law as the Law of Inertia, because it means that if something is stationary, it tends to remain stationary, and if something is moving, it tends to remain moving. The same applies to people. If you do nothing, you are likely to remain inactive, but if you are already taking action, you are able to keep on taking action, you will be able to keep on taking action.

The proof of this is in the saying: if you want something done, ask a busy person!

 **Channel Hop**

The Success Formula

And now for some maths . . . (It's easier than you think!)

The Success Formula
(Goals + Focus) x Action = Result

We know that in order to achieve results, we need a focus (personal vision) and goals.

We also know that we need action to make it happen. But take a look at the formula, and you'll see that goals and focus are *multiplied* by action. This means that the bigger the action, the bigger your results are likely to be. It also means, however, that if you don't take any action, you will never gain success, because multiplying by zero always creates zero. In other words, if you do nothing, nothing will happen. Harsh but true.

Reality Bite

Starting secondary school means lots of change: a new environment, a new school, new teachers, new subjects and new friends. I attended a small rural primary school with around fifty pupils: there were just three other boys in my class. My secondary school, on the other hand, was a much bigger vocational school, with at least six hundred pupils.

On the first day in secondary school, all first-years were given a number of tests to determine the class each student went into. Students were streamed in accordance with ability, into classes 1A, 1B, 1C, 1D or 1E. For some reason, the order of ability went from A to B to C, then to E, and finally to D. 1D didn't do the full range of subjects, and in the school yard, the 'D' stood for 'dunce'.

Having perceived myself as being at least of good average ability in primary school, I didn't give much thought or preparation to these tests, because I was confident that I would do OK. Imagine my disappointment and shock to be put into 1E – one of the lowest classes in the school! No potential Einsteins were immediately evident in 1E, that was for sure.

The class you had in your first year largely charted your academic journey through the school. It determined the subjects you were taught (or not) and the level at which those subjects were taken. We know that our performance largely matches the expectations which are set for us, and I knew, even at this stage, that it would be a struggle for me to excel. Of course, my self-image suffered – as, I am sure, did the self-image of most of the other students in the class. I was deemed to be among the weakest students in first year. What hope did I have of academic success? My school, my family and my friends now believed I was academically weak. Were they right? Or could I prove them wrong?

Thankfully, at some stage I decided to reject the negative references to my academic ability, and I decided to set my own goals: to be the best I could be. I began to work consistently, and I was moved up classes. My Junior Certificate results were good, and although I didn't take many subjects at higher level, neither did anyone in my class: only the top class in the school did that.

After the results came out, my maths teacher suggested that I take higher level maths for my Leaving Certificate. Having been in such weak classes, I didn't really believe I had the ability to do that, but, with some encouragement, I began the higher maths course. Incredibly, I found that it wasn't impossible! In fact, I could generally keep up with the remainder of the class, even though I hadn't taken the course before. For the first time in my school life, I was sitting among the top students in the school and was performing as well as them – and better than many of them. I worked hard, but I enjoyed it. The harder the problems, the greater the satisfaction I got from solving them. Maths was fun! My new-found confidence spilled over into other subjects, and I set myself high targets for my final exams. I started to believe that I could do well. I developed study plans. I worked hard and consistently. And it paid off.

In the end, just six students in the school took higher-level maths that year; I was one of them. I got one of the best grades and one of the best overall set of results in the school. I was even awarded a medal for my achievements!

From being a student who was deemed to be one of the weakest in first year, I got one of the best results not only in the school but in the county. That taught me a very valuable lesson: where you will be tomorrow is determined by the actions you take today, not by **where you are** today. Action is essential. It is rarely ability, but action, attitude and persistence that determines success.

I am currently completing my second masters degree, having already achieved first-class honours at both undergraduate- and masters-degree level. Students in 1E were never meant to do that!

*Philip is a director of **The Super Generation** and co-author of*
Make It Happen

Get in the Habit

Often, the difference between people who succeed and those who don't lies in their habits. We use the word 'habit' to mean something we do automatically, without thinking about it. Some of us have really obvious habits such as going out every Friday night, or picking our nose. (We didn't say they had to be good habits!) But as well as habits that are easily noticed, we also have habits of thought that we rarely notice. These might be things like believing we are no good at something, or laughing off compliments. If we thought about it, we would probably have no idea why we had this particular habit: it's just something we've done day after day until it becomes . . . well, a habit. The good news is that, unlike a nun, you can change your habits. Just because you procrastinate or are always late, for example, does not mean that you cannot alter your behaviour and your beliefs to get rid of these habits.

Press the Red Button ▶

Create an Action Plan

Remember how you eat an elephant one bite at a time? Well, just as we separated our personal vision into goals, we can separate our goals into actions or tasks that are then simpler and easier to execute. By creating a step-by-step plan for each goal, you can make the process easier and simpler, until you are progressing with such ease that you'll forget you ever thought it was going to be hard work. Use the space below, or get a diary or a notepad, and construct your plan with these aims in mind:

1. **Tackle one goal at a time**

   Don't overwhelm yourself by creating action plans for half a dozen goals. Not only will you be spending all your time planning and no time doing, but you will also create such a huge list of things to do that even the most capable mind would implode at the sight of it. Tackle one goal and one action plan at a time, and then reward yourself for the success of achieving that goal before you move on to the next one. (Keep reading your goals cards for the next couple of goals, so that your superconscious can start preparing for them.)

2. Make your steps and timeframe realistic

For example, you may want to decorate your whole bedroom in one day, but physical limitations mean that it's just not possible to do so. You can't make paint dry any quicker than nature wants it to, so don't set yourself up for failure by creating unachievable tasks. If you do, you'll feel down and may want to quit. On the other hand, if you set yourself achievable tasks and complete them on time, you will feel a sense of achievement and purpose that will carry you on towards your goal.

3. Appreciate your milestones and reward your achievements

As you complete each task, recognise your achievement as a milestone towards your goal. It is important to feel good about what you are doing, and to appreciate that you are working hard by rewarding yourself for your steps to success. This will drive your superconscious to keep working until you achieve your ultimate goal (More on this coming up!)

4. Take time every day to work towards your goal

Doing something every day (no matter how small) creates a new habit that allows you to progress quickly towards your dream. By making time to work on your action plan, you are not only making progress by completing tasks, but also telling your superconscious that what you are doing is important and worthwhile. This will help you become more open to external opportunities and speed up your success.

5. Have fun with your tasks

Ideally, if you are passionate about the dream you are pursuing, you will enjoy the tasks that will help you get there. Sometimes, however, there will be things that aren't such fun to do, but you can always take pleasure in the fact that you are progressing towards your goal. This is your vision and you are the creator of your success.

If you constructed an action plan for the goals in the previous episode, it might look like this:

Goal	Action Steps	Action Date
It is now December 2012 and I am a member of a band.	I will take one music lesson.	Starting this week
	I will practise for thirty minutes a day, four days a week.	Starting this week
It is now July 2013 and I have made ten new friends.	I will join two school clubs, taking on some responsibility in each one.	October 2012
	I will initiate conversation with at least three new people each week.	Weekly
	I will make sure I am in my best mood every day.	Daily
It is now September 2012, and I have spot-free skin.	I will research the best cleansing products available on the market.	This week
	I will do extra housework for my mother in order to earn the money to pay for the cleansing products.	Next three weeks
	I will use the cleansing product every day.	Daily

Reality Bite

We know Oprah Winfrey as a global American celebrity. She is a famous writer, reporter, actress, producer, activist and television talk-show host. She is undoubtedly successful – and undeniably rich. But Oprah didn't just fall into this success: she had to take action.

As a child, Oprah lived with her mother in Mississippi. When she was nine years old, she was sexually assaulted by a cousin;

she was later molested by a male friend of her mother's and by an uncle. Unable to tell anyone about the abuse she was suffering, Oprah expressed her pain and anger by repeatedly running away and getting into trouble.

Her mother wanted to put Oprah into a detention home but, because the home was full, she was sent to live with her father in Nashville. Oprah continued with her wild and promiscuous behaviour. At the age of fourteen she became pregnant, but the baby boy was stillborn.

The death of her baby devastated Oprah. Suddenly she saw that she needed to make changes in her life and to take action in order to make it a success. With the help of her father, she turned her life around, rekindling her passion for reading and getting consistently high grades at school. Aged nineteen, she got her first job – as a reporter for a radio station in Nashville. Shortly afterwards, she entered university to pursue a career in radio and television. In 1986, Oprah started **The Oprah Winfrey Show**. The rest, as they say, is history.

Listen Up

'You don't have to be great to start, but you do have to start to be great.'

Motivational speaker Zig Ziglar

Getting Started and Keeping Going

Even if we have prepared our car for the journey, and mapped out the route to our destination, we turn the key in the ignition, we will have no chance of going anywhere. Sometimes, though, getting started is the hardest part. Look again at Newton's Law of Inertia: 'An object at rest remains at rest unless acted on by an unbalanced force.' Well, now is the time to apply that force. Just as it takes one big push to get a swing going, so it needs a big push of effort and faith to begin your action plan. But remember: once you get started, you will find it easy to keep going. Honestly.

Start

Patrick Collison is an Irish scientist and company director. This is even more impressive when you know that Patrick is only in his early twenties.

At the age of eight, Patrick enrolled on his first computer course. Two years later he began to learn to program computers. By the time he was fifteen, Patrick was working on artificial intelligence projects and finished as the individual runner-up at the 40th Young Scientist and Technology Exhibition.

Like so many of our success stories, Patrick did not give up and returned to the 41st Young Scientist and Technology Exhibition with a new project, where he was awarded first prize. From there he went on to set up a software company with his younger brother, moving to California's Silicon Valley after being unable to gain funding in Ireland.

Once in America, Patrick and his brother John teamed up with some Oxford graduates and formed Auctomatic. Twelve months later, they sold the company, becoming overnight millionaires as well as internationally recognised computer scientists.

Listen Up

'A journey of a thousand miles begins with a single step.'

Lao-tzu Chinese philosopher

Reward Yourself

Once you start on the journey, you will begin to make achievements along the way. Some will be big and some will be less obvious, but they all contribute to the destination of your personal vision and are all worthy of praise and reward.

Like we mentioned in the Red Button exercise to create an Action Plan, it is important to recognise each milestone as you progress to success. By acknowledging your achievements you will feel more positive and geared up to continue working through your goals. Rewarding yourself, however subtly contributes to your superconscious' belief that you are heading in the right direction - and it feels good too!

Often we only think about giving ourselves rewards, like a chocolate bar, or a trip to a movie perhaps, once we have completed the task we've been working on. This will help with the superconscious' desire to keep going, but if you really want to max out on drive and determination, the best way to use rewards it to decide them *before* you begin your task.

Tech Specs

Impulse Control & Marshmallows

Setting yourself rewards not only gives you something nice to aim for whilst you're working on your goal, it also helps to increase your ability for achievement. Waiting for a reward implements our self-control, because we are forcing ourselves to wait for something pleasant. People who lack the ability to wait for a reward often lack the skills necessary to persevere with other events in their lives, whilst those who have greater impulse control are likely to be better adjusted, more dependable and more able to embrace and pursue challenges.

In the 1960s a psychological experiment was conducted by Walter Mischel to see if the ability to wait for a reward affected various personality traits later in life. His participants were four year old children who were given a marshmallow and then offered an agonising choice: wait a few minutes for the experiment leader to come back from an errand and have two marshmallows, or eat the one that's in front of you right now. At four years old that's no easy decision!

The participants of the study were then reviewed as teenagers. Interestingly, the two-thirds of children who had been able to delay gratification and wait for the experiment leader to return, showed much stronger emotional intelligence than the third who couldn't wait and ate the first marshmallow. As well as being better able to cope with life, they also continued to exhibit the ability to wait for rewards and were better able to pursue their goals.

For more information about the Marshmallow Challenge, take a look at *Emotional Intelligence* by Daniel Goleman.

So you see, there are very good reasons for taking a break after you achieve a goal and giving yourself a reward. It doesn't have to be something that costs a lot of money or takes a lot of time. Remember, it would be counterproductive to spend more time being rewarded than working on your action plan ☺. Just giving yourself some leisure time to relax and watch TV counts as a reward. In fact, when we've finished writing this chapter, a cup of tea and a chocolate biscuit is lined up to toast our achievement!

When you write out your action plan, why not add a column to list your rewards in? Knowing what reward you are working towards will spur you on and help keep you positive. Don't forget, it's good to treat yourself - you'll be a better person for it!

Staying Positive

As we mentioned in Episode 3, all journeys have unforeseen roadblocks and diversions. This is true in life as well as on the road. But it's not what happens that affects our actions and goals; it's how we deal with what happens.

Press Pause ⓘⓘ

Look at the picture. What do you see?
Is the glass half full or half empty?
If you take the view that the glass is half empty, how does that make you feel? What about it you think of it as being half full?

Channel Hop

Classic Tales

*The 1913 classic children's story **Pollyanna**, by Eleanor H. Porter, is a great example of the benefits of staying positive.*

Pollyanna Whittier is a young orphan who goes to live with her stern Aunt Polly in Vermont. Things seem to be bleak and horrid but Pollyanna has what she calls 'the Glad Game'. This game was made up by her father when, one Christmas, Pollyanna was hoping for a doll as a present in the charity missionary barrel, but all that was there was a pair of crutches. Pollyanna's father said that, rather than be miserable about not getting what she wanted, Pollyanna should be glad about the crutches because, as he put it: 'We don't need 'em!'

So Pollyanna copes with hardship by always finding something to be glad about. When her aunt punishes her by shutting her in a bare room, Pollyanna is glad for the view from the window. When she is given only bread and milk because she is late for dinner, Pollyanna is glad that she likes bread and milk.

But the great thing about Pollyanna's 'game' is that her positive influence begins to affect the rest of the town, as she teaches them to be positive about things too.

People who remain positive about their lives have a huge advantage over those who are negative. Negative people often achieve very little, while optimistic people find positive experiences even in major setbacks. And there's more. Positive, optimistic people have been proven to experience the following:

- **Superior health**
- **Greater achievement**
- **Persistence**
- **Emotional health**
- **Less stress, and**
- **Longer lifespan**

Now, who wouldn't want any – or all – of those traits? You can keep positive by looking for the 'silver lining' in every experience. If that seems impossible, remind yourself of your goal or dream, and use the technique of visualising this outcome to boost your energy and help you continue making progress towards it. You can also use the prospect of your reward to keep up morale. It also helps to surround yourself with like-minded people who will respect and nurture your actions rather than criticising you or acting as dreambusters. In short, it's up to you to access your potential as you execute your action plan and reward your achievements along the way.

So now you know the five steps to our SUPER System of success. Everything in the last four chapters has been designed specifically to help you achieve your goals and become the success you want to be. With these simple principles in place, you are ready and able to make it happen. But remember, you need to be willing to take action and to follow these steps. Only if you get started and stick with it can we guarantee that your dreams will become reality. If you've got the determination, we promise the SUPER System of success won't let you down!

But wait! Don't put the book aside just yet. We've got one last section to share with you: Tools for Success. In the remaining chapters, we'd like to give you some extra support to help you in making it happen.

Press Pause ⏸

Now we hope you have completed all the exercises in this section. Remember it is the most important part of the book. Here are some examples of SUPER systems. We have shortened them a little, just to give you an idea of what others have created.

Sandra, Age 15
See it 👁

I am working as a nurse where I can help people every day.
I live in a beautiful house near the beach with my family. I am married with three children and we are very happy. I enjoy spending time with my children and my husband.

We get to travel often and I love to work with the child soldiers charity in Uganda each summer. Helping others less fortunate gives me a great sense of gratitude.

Understand it 💡

I want to be a nurse because I love to help people. I have always been good at helping my grandmother and her friends, especially when she is ill and unable to do things for herself. I feel really good about myself when I am helping her.

I want to help the child soldiers in Uganda because I saw a documentary about how difficult their lives are. It is so sad that people my age are taken from their families and forced to do terrible things. I want to have a happy family because it makes me happy too. I think I will make a good mother.

Plan, Execute and Reward

Plan it (Goals)	Execute it (Actions)	Reward
It is now September 2014 and I am going to college to study nursing.	I will get a tutor to help me with my biology exam.	
	I will study for 1 hour each day after completing my homework.	I will spend time on Facebook once I have completed my 1 hour of study
It is now July 2012 and I am on a charity trip to work with child soldiers.	I will contact charities to find out how I can make the trip	
	I will organise three fundraising events.	
	I will enlist the help of my friends and family to run the charity events.	The trip is its own reward.

Simon, Age 14
See it

I am the owner of my own record company. We produce music for some of the best musicians in the business. I love to get up every day and help people make music.

I travel for two months each year to exotic locations, visiting all the wonders of the world.

I volunteer at my local youth centre teaching kids how to play the guitar. The work I do helps to keep them out of trouble and away from drugs and crime.

Understand it 💡

I love to write and play music. I want to spend my life in the music business. It is what I am truly passionate about.

I want to travel and learn from other cultures and see how they play music too. Owning my own business allows me to travel to lots of different places. I am willing to work hard to achieve my vision.

I want to help others as it inspires me to have an impact on them. I want my life to be an example; to encourage others to follow their passion.

Plan, Execute and Reward

Plan it (Goals)	Execute it (Actions)	Reward
It is now September 2015 and I am studying sound engineering in college.	I will organise my study space in my room instead of studying in front of the TV.	
	I will pay better attention in class each day.	I will watch TV for 1.5 hours after I have completed my study.
	I will follow my study plan of 8 hours per week.	I will take Saturday afternoons and all day Sunday to do whatever I want.
It is now July 2012 and I can play all of Jimmy Hendricks' riffs.	I will practice 6 hours per week.	
	I will organise weekly practice with my band every Saturday.	I will ask for a new guitar for my birthday.

EXECUTE AND REWARD

1. *Actions* speak louder than words.

2. Newton's *Law of Inertia*: an object at rest tends to stay at rest, while an object in motion tends to stay in motion.

3. Success formula: (Goals + Focus) x Action = Results

4. You can change *negative habits* into positive ones.

5. Create an *action plan* to help you achieve your goal:

   i)   Make your actions *realistic*,
   ii) Appreciate your *milestones*,
   iii) Work towards your goal *every day*, and
   iv) Have *fun*.

6. Take the plunge and *get started*.

7. *Reward* your achievements

8. Keep *positive*: there's always something to be glad about, and you can benefit from every experience, even the bad ones.

Up Next: SECTION 3: Some extra tools to help you achieve success

Overview

Make it Happen
A Success Guide
for Teenagers

Section 1
Introduction to
Success

Section 2
Making it Happen
The Super System

Section 3
Tools for Success

Episode 1
It's All in the Mind
Superconscious

Episode 2
Dream Big
Imagination

Episode 3
Break the Barriers
Empowerment

Episode 4
The Secret to
Success

Episode 5
See your
Success

Episode 6
Understand It

Episode 7
Plan Your Path

Episode 8
Execute and Reward

Episode 9
An Attitude of Gratitude
Gratitude

Episode 10
Use the Force
Affirmations

Episode 11
Heads or Tails
Positive Choice

Episode 12
Team Game
Friends

Episode 13
Manage
Your Thoughts

Episode 14
Talk the Talk, Walk the Walk
Communication

Episode 15
Never Say Never
Persistence

We all know that most things in life can be made easier with some tools to help us. Opening a tin of beans is a lot easier with a tin opener. Adding up a list of numbers is easier with a calculator. In the same way, following our SUPER system of success is easier if you have some tools to help you.

Each of the remaining seven chapters holds an invaluable tool to make your journey a smoother ride:

1. **Gratitude**
2. **Affirmations and Self-belief**
3. **Choice and Decision Making**
4. **Friends and Team work**
5. **Intuition**
6. **Communication**
7. **Persistence**

Sure, you can stop reading now and get started on your SUPER success route, but our advice it to take a look at what these tools can give you – not just in achieving your personal vision, but in your life in general. we want your successes to be your achievements, your personality and how you live your life. Don't just achieve success, *BE* success.

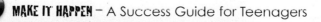

▶ Now and Next ⏺

NOW	An Attitude of Gratitude: How being grateful for the good things In your life can help positive things come to you
NEXT	Use the Force: Self-belief, affirmations and visualisation

We've already mentioned the fact that, although we may not be able to choose what happens to us in life, we can choose how we respond to it. We know that positive people experience more positive things. And one of the best ways of keeping positive is to express *gratitude*.

Listen Up

'**What you focus on expands, and when you focus on the goodness in your life, you create more of it. Opportunities, relationships, even money flowed my way when I learned to be grateful, no matter what happened in my life.**'

Oprah Winfrey

Reality Bite

Gratitude is a lesson I was taught by one of the most inspirational characters I have ever met. I travelled to Uganda with a charity called 'Zest 4 Kidz', who work with disadvantaged children all over the world. On our trip, we were to deliver a programme of music, arts and sports to a school for kids rescued from child-soldier camps. In Uganda, there is insufficient funding for a basic school curriculum, so subjects like music, art and sport are almost nonexistent.

The real purpose of the trip was to show these kids that they are not forgotten, that they are loved. they were taken

from their family and friends and forced to carry out the most unspeakable acts of violence. They had nowhere to go: their village and their families often saw them as evil because of what they had done. The children are left with nothing but horrific memories and little hope for the future.

Thankfully, the school is seen as a place of cleansing, where they can receive not only an education but also a kind of forgiveness for what they have done. Many return to their family and friends following their time there.

One of the kids stood out for me on the trip. Najja had gone through some of the most horrible experiences imaginable. Abducted from his village, he was taken to the child-soldier camp. In order to indoctrinate them into their system, the new kids were forced to do terrible things.

During his first few days, Najja was asked to shoot and kill one of the other kids from his village. Najja refused – but refusal was not an option. They threatened him, beat him and ordered him to do it. Again, he refused. So they took out a machete, pinned his right hand to the ground and chopped off his finger.

The next day, he was brought out again and told to shoot his friend once more. Again, he refused. Again, they held him down and chopped off another finger. Bloodied and beaten, he was taken away. The next day came, and with it the same scenario. Another refusal, another finger. This process continued: Najja continued to refuse; they went on butchering him until they had cut off all his fingers and thumbs, then his ears, nose, and finally his lips. Having given up on him, they beat him and left him to die in the ditch by the side of the road.

Thankfully, Najja was found by a local famer, who nursed him back to health and brought him to the child-soldier school that we were working in.

I met Najja and was amazed at how happy he was. His happiness was infectious: he was always smiling, joyous and enthusiastic. He loved to tell people how well he was doing in school, and his dream of becoming an accountant. He was also an amazing artist and showed me the pictures he had drawn, holding the pencil with the small stump that had once been his thumb. In spite of all that had happened to him, Najja was the life and soul of the classroom.

During my time there, I found the courage to ask him how he was always so happy. Knowing his story, I asked him how he could get up every day and be so joyous.

He stopped for a moment, then he looked at me and said: 'Every day I wake up, I feel so grateful. I am so lucky to be alive. Many of the kids I know will never get the opportunities I have. Many of my friends have died, and many more are still forced to fight. I am thankful to be here. I am grateful for my life.'

I was astonished. Despite the horrendous experiences Najja had gone through, he is happy because he is grateful. He is a real inspiration. Now, every time I am down or feel like complaining, I think of Najja and his attitude. Then I think of something I am grateful for, and I become happy too.

Zest4Kidz is the nominated charity of The Super Generation
Padraig is managing director of **The Super Generation** and
co-author of **Make It Happen**

Press the Red Button ▶

Feeling Grateful

Even though we want to feel gratitude, sometimes it's hard to know what to be grateful for. This exercise will give you an instant list of things to appreciate in your life. Remember, you do not have to be grateful for huge things: you might just appreciate sunny weather, or the bus arriving on time.

1. **List five things that make you happy in your life:**

2. **List five people who have helped you in the past:**

3. **List five people whom you have helped in the past:**

4. Look at your lists and appreciate all of these things, and how they have given you happiness.

Some people like to do this exercise every day – in fact, we recommend it! Get yourself a book to keep your lists in, and label it your 'Gratitude Journal'. Each day, you can write down the things that have made you grateful that day – a bit like a diary, but only for positive feelings. When you are feeling miserable, you can read back over your entries, and suddenly you will have plenty of things to feel grateful for!

Reality Bite

I taught technical drawing for a number of years and remember Stephen, a new student, in the school. I found it difficult to understand him, but I put that down to not having an ear for his accent. He was a top student: one of those people who knows what he wants and works hard to achieve it. He had plenty of natural ability, but it was his effort, work and determination that set him apart. I was sure he would get a good grade.

The parent-teacher meeting was approaching. It was not unusual for some of the less motivated students to give me advice on what I should say to their parents. They would hang about after class and then say things like: 'I got 50 percent in my last two tests, so I am improving. Make sure you tell my parents that!' Or: 'I did my homework this week, so getting it done is no longer a problem. You will tell them that, won't you?'

So I was surprised to see Stephen hanging back one day after class – even more so when I heard him ask me what I was going to tell his mother at the parent-teacher meeting. I responded that I would tell her he had a great attitude and loads of ability, and that he would get a top grade.

Stephen was amazed. 'Will you really tell her that?'

'Why wouldn't I?'

Then Stephen told me that technical drawing was the only subject he excelled in. He had dyslexia and a hearing condition: he struggled with all his other subjects. In fact, most people who had his condition are never able to speak at all, so it was remarkable that I understood him as well as I did. Stephen didn't speak until he was five years old, and those early years of isolation meant that, as a child, he often found it hard to interact with others. Apparently, both his doctors and the various schools he attended gave up on him. Stephen's mother was the only person who supported him and believed in him.

Now that Stephen had discovered his talent for technical drawing, he desperately wanted to share it with his mother. He knew that if I told her how well he was doing, she would believe me. By proving that he was a success, Stephen would be giving something back to his mother after all her years of support.

Stephen's faith and gratitude towards his mother was inspirational. Given his appetite for work, and his grateful and optimistic attitude, I reckon that Stephen will have plenty of opportunities throughout his life to show his mum that her faith in him has been rewarded.

Philip is a director of **The Super Generation** *and co-author of* **Make It Happen**

Being Grateful Brings Success

Having gratitude is not only about being aware of the good things in life, but also about appreciating those things. Being grateful rather than being negative alters how we see the world, so that we begin to see things positively. And when we see things positively, we tend to attract positive opportunities. And positive opportunities bring success and achievement.

When we see things positively, we can attract positive opportunities that will bring success and achievement.

People who are grateful get more out of life, because they see more solutions than setbacks. They have more energy, and are happier than people who dwell on the miserable side of life. But expressing gratitude is a habit that most people need to learn, and it's all too easy just to say 'Yeah, OK, I'm grateful', and move on to the next thing in your life. If you really want to see the benefits that being grateful can bring, you need to convince your superconscious to become grateful too. That's why keeping a gratitude journal helps: every time you write in it, you are repeating the message of gratitude. Eventually, being grateful will become a habit.

Psychologists Robert Emmons and Mike McCullough were aware that gratitude is the 'forgotten factor' in research about happiness. They decided to look at how gratitude affects people's health and well-being. Guess what they found out?

- People who keep a gratitude journal feel better physically and emotionally than those who use a diary to write about negative feelings or general life events. They are also less envious of other people's material possessions.

- People who make lists of things they are grateful for are more likely to have a positive attitude and make progress towards personal goals.

- Taking time each day to be grateful makes you more alert, enthusiastic, determined and attentive, as well as giving you more energy. It can also help you sleep better.

- People who believe in gratitude are generally more generous and helpful to others. This could be because they find it easier to imagine how other people are feeling.

Remember: grateful people don't deny or ignore the negative aspects of life – they just focus on the positive!

Listen Up

'On longitude or latitude, my attitude is gratitude!'
From a sketch by Victoria Wood

Reality Bite

Like most people, I have been faced with some truly awful challenges in my life: depression, losing a sister at a young age, and the painful ending of a twenty-one-year relationship, to name a few. None of these have been easy to deal with or work through, but I can honestly say that my saviour at some of life's lowest points has definitely been gratitude.

During one of these times, a close friend introduced me to a daily gratitude routine, which I do now as naturally as brushing my teeth. And just like brushing my teeth, there are occasions where I've forgotten to do it, but my teeth haven't fallen out, and I am no less of a person for not doing my list for a night.

Now it may sound complicated, but trust me, it's not. It is also a technique which is:

a) easy to remember

b) private, and

c) has no fees attached, no matter how often you use it.

So, let me explain how this works for me. I simply give thanks at the end of the day for a minimum of three things. These three things don't need to be earth-shatteringly amazing; they can be as simple as: 'I give thanks for not drinking Diet Coke, because I know it's full of unhealthy things and is probably burning away a layer of my stomach as we speak.'

Last night, I gave thanks that my children and I were in our beds, warm, with a roof over our heads – which for me, as single mum, is a huge blessing. I also gave thanks for getting to spend time with my pregnant friend and her delicious baby girl. Then, lastly, for finding the time and inspiration to do some writing, which feeds my body in a far healthier way than any fizzy juice ever could.

But . . . there are nights when I have had very challenging days at work or in my private life, where I dig deep and always, always find something to be grateful for. In doing this, I feel that I am going to sleep with something positive in my head on the most negative days.

Like thinking when my sister died: 'I am so grateful Mary knew and loved my children unreservedly before she died. My children are better people for having her in their lives.'

Or on nights when I felt upset after my separation, I had thoughts like: 'I am grateful to have had this space to explore a new life on my own. I just have to get used to being a solo traveller again.'

Then, after the disastrous interview for a job I was convinced I wanted, I gave thanks for the chance to explain how good I was in my current job, and realised that actually I enjoyed my work enough to stay put.

Sometimes in life things are so far out of our control that we find it difficult to see positive outcomes. It's at these points, and on the most challenging days, that I give thanks for the tiniest things, like tiny fragile flowers growing through eight inches of cement, or one luminous white cloud on a day when the sky appeared to have a burst water main, or being able to walk home after a bad meeting with my boss. I live on a hill, and am grateful to have the energy to get up it unaided.

Life can feel like we are struggling up a hill, but if you remember to be grateful for the things you see and experience on your journey, you can't help but appreciate all you have, and are.

Katie is a single mum and a reiki practitioner

Ways to Become More Grateful

As well as being grateful for the things that happen in our lives, and taking time to reflect on them, there are other habits we can acquire – or change – to make us feel more grateful. Like any habit, these will need to be repeated regularly to make them stick in your superconscious.

1) Don't make comparisons

It's easy to look at someone else and wish that you had their body, their car, their money, or even their entire life. Often things seem great for other people, and hard for you. This is rarely the case, though, and comparing yourself to other people is likely to lead to you have negative feelings about yourself and, often, about them too. Keep in mind that you have your unique life and they have theirs: you wouldn't compare an apple and a banana, so why compare two people?

If you find yourself wishing that your life was more like someone else's, stop for a moment and ask yourself what aspects of your own life someone else might envy. Be grateful that you have these things in your life, and remember that there will always be someone in the world who is less fortunate than yourself (and often they are closer than you think).

2) Find a flip side

Like the story of Pollyanna in Episode 7, whenever you are feeling negative about something, try and find the positive flip side. You may be disappointed that you didn't score the winning goal in your hockey match, but you can be glad that someone on your team did. If all else fails, you can feel grateful that you have the ability to feel grateful!

3) Appreciate nature

The world around us is always something to be grateful for. Whenever you get the chance, appreciate the amazing natural world: the sea, forests, landscapes. If you take a five-minute walk, you will see dozens of things to be grateful for. Be grateful for the diversity of living things on the planet, and appreciate your part in the universe.

4) Let things go

If something is bothering you and getting you down, just let it go. There is no benefit in getting cross and uptight about a situation, especially if it is out of your control. Perhaps you feel that you could have done better in an exam . . . One thing is for sure: worrying about it won't change the result you got. Take a breath, acknowledge that your negative feelings aren't helping, and let them fade away. Then choose something to be grateful for, and you'll soon feel positive again.

5) Forgive and forget

If you've been hurt by someone, don't let your negative feelings about the situation take over. Carrying negativity around will prompt your superconscious to start looking for more, and this will begin to colour how you see the world. Although it's not always easy, try to find a reason to understand the situation from another viewpoint and let the negativity go. After all, you're the only one who's getting hurt. Once it's gone, move on. Being positive brings its own rewards; don't let someone else spoil your day.

Reality Bite

My grand-uncle was a typical old man. He loved to complain, and always found fault. Nothing was ever good enough. Apart from that, you couldn't help but love him.

His name was David, but everyone called him Tuss. I referred to him as Uncle Tuss. He was a genius with his hands, whether it was doing the electrics, woodwork or plumbing.

I went everywhere with Tuss. I have very fond memories of him. He was a religious man; when he did the church collection, I used to help him count the money. Then he was involved in the local drama society, and I used to help him make the props. He was also good at cooking. I loved the way he cooked chicken: it was more moist than my mother's.

We both liked birds. When I won a project on garden birds in primary school, Tuss made some fantastic bird houses for me.

By the time I was eighteen, I wasn't hanging around with him much. I was doing what people of that age do. He didn't like it – and let me know it.

'I hear you're up the street drinking porter. Hmm,' he proclaimed one afternoon. That was his way of saying he disapproved.

That summer was wet: it rained nearly every day. I had worked for my dad all summer, to save money for college. He gave me the last week off, and for some reason I decided to spend it with Tuss. We spent the week painting his bird-houses. The sun shone, and over the tins of paint and varnish we chatted about anything and everything. We had a great time. My friends thought it was strange that I spent so much time with him, but I was really enjoying his company. On the last day of the holidays, my friends prised me away from him to go swimming.

As we cycled to the end of my road on the way back from swimming, I saw cars parked outside Tuss's house. I knew there was something wrong: my stomach knotted. The neighbours had gathered, and the house was thronged. Tuss had collapsed in the shed that afternoon.

At the funeral, all I could think about was our bird-houses. I was so grateful for that last week we spent together: our mutual love of nature and craft had brought us back together. I had learned so much from him. He was a good man, and always tried to do the right thing. I still miss him today, but when I feel sad I recall the times we spent together, and my gratitude always makes me feel better.

Ray is an entrepreneur and trainer with **The Super Generation**

Gratitude Meditation

When you've had a bad day and everything seems hopeless, try this exercise to bring back your positive energy.

1. Sit quietly, close your eyes and breathe deeply.
2. Begin to reflect on your day, and let the things that you are grateful for come into your conscious mind. If you need something to focus on, think about your family and friends, or your health, or what you have in your life that other people who are less fortunate than you do not have. Think of five things you are grateful for.
3. With each thing that you think of, let the feeling of gratitude grow within you. Let it build up until you feel really happy with life and the way you see the world. Smile.
4. Now open your eyes and take this feeling of gratitude with you to your next task of the day.

Reality Bite

New York City is an amazing place. The first time I was there, I was really excited: just seeing the skyline was amazing. I planned to do everything I could to experience as much of the city as possible during my short stay. In New York, the movies become reality: places I had previously only heard about, like the Empire State Building, Times Square and Central Park, were right there in front of my eyes. On looking at Statue of Liberty on Ellis Island, I couldn't help thinking about the tens of thousands of Irish people who had arrived in America hoping to achieve liberty and freedom.

I was staying in a hostel on the Upper East Side of the city, near Harlem. Hostels are great places to meet other people, to exchange stories of travels and to plan for the days and nights ahead. One evening, one of the travellers I had become friendly with said that he was going to do some volunteer work in a soup kitchen the following day. At first, I wasn't sure what that was about! At that time, there were a lot of homeless people in

New York: there seemed to be a constant stream of them checking the bins for scraps. My rule was to avoid eye contact with them: I had never had any desire to speak to any of them. My friend suggested that he wanted to see the 'other side of New York', and wondered if I would be interested in joining him. I agreed, but reluctantly, and with some trepidation.

On my way to the soup kitchen, I was hoping that I would be put working in the kitchen: that way, I wouldn't have to have contact with the homeless people. When we arrived, there were already around a hundred people lined up outside. I got nervous: all the negative connotations I had about the homeless came to my mind. And my hope of working in the kitchen was soon dashed. The manager in charge said that all newcomers served food in the dining area. So I would be feeding the homeless – but I was assured that we would all be perfectly safe. Nonetheless, I was worried that we would be feeding drunks – mad, angry men. In fact, my experience was very different.

I met Frank, a former accountant in his forties, who was homeless. I thought that if you work hard, you get a well-paid job and have an easy life. Frank was definitely an exception to this rule. But the room was full of exceptions: so many of the people there had once had good jobs, but bad things had happened to them. I was told that Frank's marriage had broken down, and that he'd subsequently become dependent on alcohol and lost his job. He was now a regular at the soup kitchen.

Then someone heard my accent and asked if I was from Ireland. I started chatting to the man, who was called Seán, and found out he had left Ireland in the early 1960s and had spent many years living and working in America. Then he became ill, lost his job and became homeless. He had lost all hope of finding another job. He was not bitter or angry: in fact, he was very grateful for what he was receiving. He had developed a friendship with the owner of a bakery, who provided him with leftovers every evening. He said that, because of his friendship with the bakery owner, he was never hungry, and he was grateful for that.

Working in the soup kitchen that day taught me a lot. For one thing, my view of the homeless changed forever. For the first time, it became clear to me that anyone could find themselves homeless. I will never forget how grateful Seán felt towards the *baker. Seán certainly made me more grateful for many things in my life that I had previously taken for granted.*

*Philip is a director of **The Super Generation** and co-author of **Make It Happen***

The more time you spend promoting feelings of gratitude in yourself, the less time there is to have negative thoughts. Soon you will become a much more positive person, and you will begin to attract positive things into your life. This not only helps you on your road to finding success and achieving your goals, but it also makes you a great person to be around. Your friends and family will notice a difference in you, and you will probably become more grateful as a person.

60 Seconds

An Attitude of Gratitude

1. Having gratitude helps us to be aware of and appreciate the good things in our life.

2. When we see things positively, we can attract positive opportunities, which will bring success and achievement.

3. People who are grateful get more out of life, because they see more solutions than setbacks.

4. Make gratitude a habit by keeping a gratitude journal.

5. There are scientific benefits to being grateful: more energy, better health, and so on.

6. Ways to have more gratitude:
   i)   Don't make comparisons
   ii) Find a flip side
   iii) Appreciate nature
   iv) Let things go, and
   v)   Forgive and forget.

Up Next: Use the Force: Self-belief, affirmations and visualisation

Now and Next 📺

NOW	**Use the Force: How tapping into the strength that's inside you can boost you on your way to success**
NEXT	**Heads or Tails: Choices and decision-making**

Here are some fabulous tools for helping you with the S in our SUPER System. Self-belief, affirmations and visualisation are all key to help you really SEE YOUR SUCCESS.

Channel Hop 📱

The Y Factor

It's Saturday night . . . It's live . . . It's The Y Factor!

A young girl dressed in a tutu and four-inch heels sways out onto the stage and drawls into the mike. 'Hey there. My name's Sasha Smithers. I'm going to sing "Nothing's gonna stop me".'

She coughs loudly and tugs at her skirt, before taking hold of the microphone and launching into a song that sounds like a parrot being strangled by a chainsaw.

The judges look at each other and raise their eyebrows. The stern-looking man at the end raises a hand and, reluctantly, Sasha stops singing.

'Sorry love,' he says in clipped tones. 'I'm afraid something **is** *going to stop you: me.'*

'But I hadn't finished,' Sasha whines miserably.

'No, but your singing career has,' the man retorts swiftly. 'Take it from me when I say that you can't sing.'

'But . . . '

'No buts, darling. It's time to return to the day job.'

The members of the panel smile to each other as she leaves, *and they make jokes about the standard of this year's contestants. At home, we sit watching in disbelief as Sasha tells the presenters backstage that she will be back next year – that she **will** be famous. Why, we ask ourselves, would anyone go on television and do that? Perhaps that's the reason it's called* **The Y Factor . . .**

Odd as it may seem, these singers have something we all need: self-belief. Even though they may not make it as a singer, their self-belief will ultimately lead to them being successful: when they discover their real talent, they will uncover their true potential. Often, we have to try many things before we find what we are really good at, or what we really enjoy. If we approach everything with the self-belief that was shown by the girl on *The Y Factor*, we will increase our chances of success exponentially.

Self-belief is about having absolute certainty in your own potential.

Someone who believes in themselves doesn't worry about what other people think of them, or panic about whether they are good enough. It's as though they have super powers! And these super powers will help them to combat self-belief's arch-rival, self-doubt.

Self-belief is having absolute certainty in your own potential.

The Misdeeds of Doubt

Most of us are not naturally filled with absolute certainty about who we are and what we do. Instead, most of us are accompanied in life by a little demon called doubt. Now, doubt can be very useful: it helps us to consider right from wrong and can prevent us from coming to harm.

For example, if you were thinking about jumping off a ten-foot-high wall, doubt would quite sensibly suggest to you that you could hurt yourself. And so, as we grow up, we begin to listen to doubt to help us make decisions. The problem is, we can become over-dependent on his advice and start questioning ourselves about things that have nothing to do with doubt at all. In short, we begin to doubt ourselves.

Self-belief VS. Doubt

Self-doubt is the enemy of self-belief. Say that your goal is to get into university. Over the previous episodes, you have spent time planning your goals, setting yourself tasks and building your passion so that you really want to get into university. You want to be a student, and study and have fun with new mates. You can feel the excitement about reaching your goal building up inside you, helping you make your dream come true. And then, when you're not looking, doubt whispers in your ear: 'You're not really clever enough though, are you?'

Self-doubt is the enemy of self-belief.

It's as though someone has thrown cold water over you, and your excitement fades away. You start to question yourself further: Are you clever enough to go? Will you pass your exams? What if no one likes you?

From being a helpful lodger in your mind, doubt has become an unwelcome guest, spreading himself around and putting out your dreams. Every time you try to build up your desire, doubt will come along and put the fire out.

But don't worry: your self-belief is tougher than you think!

'If you hear a voice within you say "You cannot paint", then by all means paint, and that voice will be silenced.'

Vincent Van Gogh

Final exams in school are always a lot of pressure. You work hard for years, and it all comes down to a few three-hour exams that dictate your future. My final exams turned out to be a disaster. My best subjects were maths and physics, and I had pinned all my hopes on these two subjects, with the intention to study engineering, but I made a complete mess of the exams.

I was hoping for an 'A', or at least a 'B', in both. However, I ended up with a 'C' and a 'D'. It was a crushing blow. I had worked hard, but my results were terrible. In the end, I did not get on any of the courses I'd wanted to do: I had dreams of studying in some of the best universities in the country, but none of them offered me a place.

I was offered a diploma course, and felt I had little choice but to take it. As a result of my poor results, I started to believe I was a poor student, and not very intelligent. During the next three years, I really struggled with the exams: I eventually failed the course, and left with nothing.

My beliefs were now ingrained: academic study was not for me. Years before, I had decided to become an engineer, but that dream was starting to fade.

I worked for a few years, but with no qualifications I was paid very poorly. Even though I worked hard, I struggled to make money and never had enough of it to do the things I really wanted to do. The life I had dreamed about seemed a very long way off.

Although those years were tough, they led me to start changing my beliefs. I worked in an engineering company, as the lowest-paid office assistant, watching and helping the engineers. I saw what they were doing and began to feel: 'I can do that.' I saw no reason why I couldn't do the job as well if not better than they did. It made me determined to go back to college and get my engineering qualifications.

I went back part-time, making a four-hour round trip three times a week to go to night classes. It was hard, but I kept telling myself: 'I can do this. I believe I can do this.' I also read about how other people studied and prepared for exams. I learned about mind mapping, speed reading and memory techniques. I focused on doing practice exams and regular reviews.

Four years later, I graduated with a first-class honours degree. Shortly after that, I went on to complete a masters degree at a prestigious business school. I graduated fourth in a class of some of the smartest and best engineers in the country. It was a fantastic achievement. I had gone from a student who failed to a student who was graduating near the top of the class.

Hard work was obviously an important part of what I achieved, but the real secret to my success was changing my self-belief. I went from thinking 'I can't' to believing 'I can'. And I did.

*Padraig is lead trainer and managing director with **The Super Generation** and co-author of **Make It Happen***

Gaining Self-belief

As we've said in earlier episodes, your state of mind is created by the repetition of instructions to your superconscious. Then, your thoughts are translated into a physical reality. All thoughts, positive or negative, will influence your superconscious mind. Fortunately, we know we can train our mind to believe what we want it to believe. We can get rid of negative thoughts and replace them with positive ones, so that our superconscious develops unbreakable self-belief. The great thing is that once we believe in ourselves, other people believe in us too. And when we are not questioning ourselves or our abilities, neither is our superconscious. This makes achieving our goals and desires much less difficult.

Poetry Corner

If you *think* you are beaten, you are,
If you *think* you dare not, you don't
If you like to win, but you *think* you can't,
It is almost certain you won't.

If you *think* you'll lose, you're lost,
For out of the world we find,
Success begins with a fellow's will –
It's all in the *state of mind*.

If you *think* you are outclassed, you are,
You've got to *think* high to rise,
You've got to be *sure of yourself*
Before you can ever win a prize.

Life's battles don't always go
To the stronger or faster man,
But sooner or later the man who wins
Is the man *who thinks he can!*
Napoleon Hill

Affirmations Made Easy

We know we need to think positively and have self-belief, but how do we do it? Well, although most of the information that goes into our superconscious is generated automatically, we can actively control what thoughts we want to believe by using affirmations. An affirmation is a statement about something we want to achieve that we would like to become part of our state of mind, so that we believe it effortlessly.

Replay 🔄

An affirmation is a statement about something we want to achieve that we would like to become part of our state of mind so that we believe it effortlessly.

You've used affirmations already, when we asked you to write a goal statement. Goals can be about what you want to achieve, or have already achieved. For example: 'It is now December 2011, and I can play the guitar.' Goals are also an important way of helping you think about the type of person you would like to become, and increasing your self-belief. For example: 'It is now March 2012 and I feel more assertive.' These affirmations help you increase your confidence and remove any inner doubt that might be lurking.

Reality Bite 👤❗

When I first learned of 'affirmations', I have to admit I was a little sceptical. How could simply saying a few words out loud (or at least in your own head) make any difference? Plus, wouldn't you look a little crazy walking around talking to yourself all the time?

Then I started to realise that everyone talks to themselves all the time. We have full-blown conversations with that little voice in the back of our mind. (By the way, if you're reading this and saying 'I don't have a little voice in the back of **my** mind' – well, it was the little voice I'm talking about that just said that to you!)

So how did I start to use affirmations? Well, I've taken up golf again recently, and have been trying to improve my game. I learned how to play as a young teenager but then gave up for a few years. Some days, I play well; other days not so good. Often how I got on over the first few holes dictated how well I played that day.

During a recent game, my day started badly. Nothing was going right. Every shot I hit was terrible, and I started to get really self-conscious. Was everybody looking at me? Were they laughing at how badly I was playing? Then things got worse and worse. Every time I stepped up to hit a ball, I could hear myself saying: 'It's going to go wrong again. Why am I even bothering today? It's just another bad day.'

Then I remembered about positive affirmations. I remembered that all the top sports people use them in some shape or form. So I started to say to myself: 'I'm a great golfer.' To be honest, it felt a bit strange. First, I'm not a great golfer, by any standard, and second, how would saying those words to myself make any difference? But my game couldn't get any worse, so I kept repeating the words to myself.

I stepped up to hit the next ball, on the sixth tee. I concentrated hard, but nothing happened. Well, nothing **good**, anyway: the ball went miles to the left into the rough. As I walked over to find it, I kept repeating the words: 'I'm a great golfer. I'm a great golfer.' The next few shots weren't much better, but instead of complaining to myself and getting even more self-conscious, I just kept saying those words to myself. The seventh hole wasn't too good, and the eighth wasn't much better. I began thinking: 'I knew this affirmation thing was a load of rub–' but then, before I could finish that sentence, I said to myself again: 'I'm a great golfer. I'm a great golfer.' Then, on the ninth *hole, things started to turn around. For the rest of the game, I played better than I had ever done before. And it was all because I said a few simple encouraging things to myself, instead of being self-critical.*

*Padraig is managing director with **The Super Generation** and co-author of **Make It Happen***

The key to a successful affirmation is not what you've written but how often you repeat it. Repetition is the only known way to train your superconscious to believe the affirmation. The more you repeat the affirmation, the easier it becomes to convince your superconscious that you will achieve your goal.

The key to successful affirmations is repetition.

The Power of the Mind

Thanks to science, we know that our vision works upside-down. The light that comes into our eyes creates an upside-down image on the back of our eyeballs. Our mind then turns that image the right way up, to give us the correct picture of what we are looking at.

As part of an experiment, scientists gave some volunteers pairs of glasses that inverted the images they saw. When they wore them, everything looked upside-down. When they took them off, it went back to normal. But after wearing the glasses for some time, things began to look the right way up through the glasses, and upside-down without them. The mind had got used to the glasses and had learnt how to 'correct' the images.

In the same way, if we repeat our affirmations to the superconscious, eventually it will become convinced that they are true and real. This will fill you with self-belief, and your superconscious will be ready to accept and act upon any action you need to carry out in order to achieve your goal.

Goodbye, doubt; hello, success!

Me TV

Repetition is a fantastic tool, but we need to do more than just read the words aloud. Reading aloud can be boring – as we know from hours spent in English lessons listening to our classmates read from Shakespeare or Dickens. What we need is a bit of spark; a bit of pizzazz! To achieve this, you can use visualisation techniques to put images, sensations and emotions into your affirmations to help make them real.

Visualisation puts images, sensations and emotions into your affirmations to help make them real.

We've all tuned out when we've got bored with someone reading aloud from a book. Well, it's just the same for your superconscious. Although you may be reading your affirmations aloud, all your superconscious is hearing is: 'Blah, blah, blah.' Not very inspiring.

Visualisation uses three techniques to help your superconscious believe your affirmation:

1. **Images**

   When you are saying your affirmation, make it come alive in your mind. Try to see the events that are happening, and watch yourself achieving your goal. Close your eyes and imagine yourself at the cinema. See the screen in front of you, and watch your affirmation take place, just like a movie, on the screen. Make the picture really big. When you've watched it from your cinema seat, imagine climbing inside the screen and becoming part of the action yourself, until you feel as though you have already experienced your goal.

2. **Sensations**

   Of course, we don't just look at things. We also sense things through sound, touch, taste and smell. When you enter the cinema screen, look around you, and use your other senses. What can you hear? What are you touching, and how does it feel? What kind of taste do you have in your mouth? Are there any distinct smells that are associated with your goal?

3. Emotions

Finally, *feel* your affirmation. This is a great way to get rid of any self-doubt and convince your superconscious that you are confident about achieving your goals. When you climb into your cinema screen, imagine how you will feel when you have achieved your goal. How will you behave? How will your body experience the emotion? Work hard to feel good and positive about your achievement. You deserve it as much as anyone else.

If you can put these three things together, visualisation is one of the most powerful tools you can have to achieve success. When we are awake, our minds experience things, and know them to be real. What's really impressive, though, is that when we are in a deep sleep, or a state of deep relaxation, our minds have the same brain patterns as when we are awake. That's why, when we dream, it feels as though the actions taking place in the dream are really happening. And because of this great feature of our minds, we can trick our superconscious into believing that we have already achieved our goals. When you and your superconscious know how it will feel to achieve your goals, your superconscious will work out a plan to make that a reality – no questions asked!

Press the Red Button ▶

Affirmations to Improve Self-belief

Repeat, visualise and carry out the affirmations below with complete self-belief. You will soon begin to influence your thoughts and actions, and convince your superconscious to work towards your goal.

1. Reaffirm your ability

'I *know* I can achieve _____ , and I have every confidence in my success.'

2. Visualise your ideal self

'I am a great person in every way. I like the way I look and feel. I am content.'
(Now visualise your ideal self for a few minutes.)

3. Visualise your goal

'I can see myself achieving my goal. I am a success.'

MAKE IT HAPPEN – A Success Guide for Teenagers

(Now visualise your current goal for a few minutes.)

4. Personal vision statement

'I believe in my vision for my life, and know that I will achieve it.'

5. Be environmental and magnetic

'I will be open and honest to everyone I come into contact with. Helping others will bring me positive opportunities that will help me achieve my goal.'

Reality Bite

I tried everything, I really did: drinking lots of water, fasting, eating Mars bars, doing hypnosis, drinking banana milkshakes, even holding my breath for sixty seconds solid! But no matter what I tried, I always got a stitch whenever I ran. After ten or twenty minutes of intense running, it always happened: that fiery, burning sensation in the side of my abdomen, followed by a tightening of the lungs. It was a like a can-opener ripping out my stomach. To say I was in pain is putting it mildly.

It was so frustrating – especially when you are a teenager, when you should be at your sporting best. Being outsprinted, or running out of steam with ten minutes to go in a critical cup game, is not an option. Deciding that my fortune was not in football, I hung up my boots before the age of seventeen. I had come to a simple conclusion: I was no good at running.

Several years later, I was overweight, unfit and, worst of all, lazy. So I put on my running gear and went to the gym. I looked at the treadmill with terror. When I clambered on, I felt my stomach tighten, even before I'd hit the 'on' button! A few minutes later, I was sweating profusely and felt like gagging. Just short of the ten-minute mark, I called time and retreated to the jacuzzi. As I nursed my blisters, I reaffirmed to myself: I was no good at running.

Having signed up to work with a fitness trainer, I returned for more treadmill torture the next day. This session was no better.

MAKE IT HAPPEN – A Success Guide for Teenagers

Within five minutes, I had a blood vessel the size of a football sticking out of my temple. The louder I groaned, the more my trainer growled. I figured that a cardiac arrest was a better option than facing his wrath, so I kept going, saying to myself 'You're a lean, keen running machine', in an attempt to keep up my momentum.

For the next month, I toughed out the personal-training sessions, repeating my 'lean, keen' affirmation. Before I knew it, I was comfortably running for ten minutes without a break. Soon I was up to twenty minutes, then thirty. In fact, I was starting to feel healthy, and the word 'exercise' did not make me want to vomit. In fact, I actually looked forward to going to the gym.

By the end of the year, there had been two major developments: (i) I was now planning my first 10k race, and (ii) I had bought my first pair of proper running shoes. Without doubt, I had caught the running bug. I started to run every day: in the mornings, before work, and at the weekends. I even started playing football again. One weekend, I did a 10k race before togging out for the local football team. Then I played another ninety-minute match the next day! My running exploits were becoming legendary.

My thirty-minute runs turned into hour-long ones. My 10k runs turned into ten-mile ones, and my half-miles turned into half marathons. Before long, there was only one milestone left: the marathon.

The night before my first marathon, I didn't sleep a wink. As I oiled up my legs before the event, I reflected on how far I had come. As I crossed the starting line, my stomach tingled with nerves. By the ten-mile mark, I felt good. I chatted with the crowd. The atmosphere was great. By the fifteen-mile mark, I was hot, but my running was fluid. At twenty miles, things quickly changed. It felt so familiar – that burning sensation, the crippling cramp. Slowing to a crawl, my stomach literally knotted, and I felt as if I had swallowed a pile of glass. Determined not to stop, I reverted to my tried-and-trusted affirmation: 'You're a lean, keen running machine! You're a lean, keen running machine!'

At twenty miles, I grabbed a hard sweet offered up by a young girl who was cheering us on. It took me about a mile to take the wrapper off. The sweet gave me the energy I needed to push on to the finish. As I neared the line, I could feel my heart swell with pride. The crowd cheered, and I felt the strength come *back into my body. I had never felt so good! As I lay on the massage table after my run, the masseuse looked at me admiringly.*

'You're in before the crowd. You must be a good runner,' she said.

As I lay on the table, admiring my medal, I thought to myself: 'I'm a lean, keen running machine.'

Raymond is an entrepreneur and trainer with **The Super Generation**

Press the Red Button ▶

Goal-and-Self-belief Combo

Now you know how to increase your self-belief and use visual affirmations to their maximum potential, you've got an even more powerful tool for success:

1. Find a quiet place – maybe in bed at night, or in the morning – and close your eyes. Repeat the written goals you want to achieve. Make sure you state what you want, and when you will have achieved it. (Revisit Episode 6 if you want to refresh your goals.) As you say the goals out loud, visualise yourself having achieved that goal. See it. Sense it. Feel it.

2. Repeat your affirmation and visualisation every morning when you wake up, and every night before you go to sleep, until you can see and feel the goal you wish to achieve and are full of self-belief.

3. Place your goal card where you can see it before you go to bed and when you get up in the morning. (You could put it by your bedside lamp or stick it to the mirror in your bathroom.) Read it every time you see it until you have memorised it so that your superconscious can believe it.

Use the Force

1. *Self-belief* is a state of *absolute certainty* that can be achieved through affirmation and visualisation.

2. *Self-doubt* is the enemy of self-belief.

3. An *affirmation* is a statement of desire that we want to become part of our state of mind.

4. The key to effective affirmations is repetition.

5. The key to effective affirmations is repetition.

6. The key to effective affirmation is repetition.
   (See, it really *is* important.)

7. Use *visualisation* techniques, with images, sensations and emotions, to help your superconscious believe your affirmations and build your self-belief.

8. Follow these affirmations for self-belief:
   i.   reaffirm your ability
   ii.   visualise your ideal self
   iii. visualise your goal

Up Next: Making Choices and Decisions

Now and Next ⬝

NOW	Heads or Tails: How reacting positively and being empowered helps us achieve success
NEXT	Team Game: How good friends can help you make it happen

We spend our lives dealing with choices and making decisions. What shall I wear? What shall I have for breakfast? What time should I leave for school/college/work? The list goes on . . .

Sometimes, though, the choices are harder, and the decisions we make more important. Should I spend my savings? Should I go to university? Should I quit my job?

These are all external decisions, but every day we also deal with *internal* choices. Whenever something happens to us that is outside of our control, we have the choice to deal with it either positively or negatively. This episode looks at the importance of decision-making, and how we can learn to make positive choices.

Decision-making

The success guy, Napoleon Hill, found out some great stuff about decisions. He realised that the people who succeed most are those who make decisions *promptly* and *definitely*, and who change their decisions *slowly*. People who take a long time to decide on something but then change their minds quickly are more likely to fail. He realised that failure comes from lack of decisiveness.

Replay ↻

People who succeed are more likely to make decisions promptly and definitely and to change their decisions slowly.

There are a couple of reasons why this could be the case. Firstly, people who take ages to decide something often spend so long thinking about it that by the time they finally make the decision, they have no energy left to implement it. This often happens at revision time: have you ever spent so long making a revision timetable to help you decide what to study that you can't be bothered to do any revision?

Also, people who are more likely to change their minds will often do so before they've got far enough to see if their decision will be a success. Clearly, the more often you change your mind and have to start again, the longer it will take you to reach your goal.

Gut Instinct

The other reason why you're more likely to succeed if you make your decisions promptly and with certainty is to do with science. Not again, we hear you cry! Sorry, but it's true. You've probably heard about 'gut instinct', and people making decisions based on how they feel, rather than using logical arguments. Well, this has got social scientists thinking – and, more importantly, doing research. They believe that when you have a 'gut reaction' to something, it's not just last night's pizza giving you indigestion, it's your superconscious's way of letting you know what

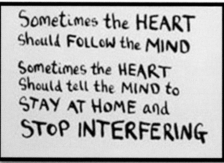

it thinks. Too often, we depend on our logical, conscious mind to work things out, when really we should listen to our superconscious, which acts much faster, and uses all the information available to it, to make a decision – which is, as a result, usually the right one.

From a cartoon by Edward Monkton

Under the Influence

If you want to make good choices in life, you need to take full responsibility for your decisions. You might think that asking your mates' opinions about your goals is a great idea to help you figure out what to do, but it doesn't always work out like that. Sometimes, if the person you are talking to does not fully understand and sympathise with your ideas, they can influence your opinion and even make you stop believing in yourself. And since we know how important self-belief is, it's

MAKE IT HAPPEN – A Success Guide for Teenagers

easy to see what a bad effect stopping believing in yourself would have on you achieving your goals.

Replay

Take responsibility: good decisions are not necessarily influenced by other people's opinions.

The problem is that society is full of things that have an influence, bad or otherwise, on us. We are surrounded by newspapers, televisions and the Internet, not to mention other people, who constantly bombard us with opinions and ideas – whether we agree with them or not. And that's fine. In fact, it can be useful to see what someone else believes, to help you think about whether or not you believe it too. But when you're making important, goal-setting, life-changing, success-building decisions, it's not the time to be swayed by other people's opinions about what you should or shouldn't do. Trust your instincts. And, if necessary, discuss things with a small group of people whom you *know* have the same feelings on the subject as you do (More on that in Episode 12.)

Press Pause ⏸

Ways to Deal with Decision-making

1. Make your decisions slowly and carefully.
2. Be confident in your decision, and stick with it.
3. Don't be unnecessarily influenced by other people's opinions.

'The world has a habit of making room for people whose words and actions show they know where they are going.'

Napoleon Hill

Choice

You're probably familiar with this children's saying: 'Sticks and stones may break my bones/ But names will never hurt me.' Now, if you've ever been called names by other kids, you'll know that that statement is not completely accurate. Being made fun of is never nice, and the hurt can last a long time. But what can you do about it? It's not as though you asked to be called 'spotty' or 'chav' or 'geek' or whatever. And it's not as though the people doing the name-calling are likely to respond well to: 'Excuse me, but would you mind not calling me names because it hurts my feelings?' So there's nothing you can do. You've got no way out. No choice. Or have you? You may not be able to choose what happens to you, but you *can* choose how you *respond* to it.

Reality Bite

Growing up on the rough streets of Queens, two young brothers could be forgiven for thinking they had no choice about their future. At the ages of 6 and 7, neither of them would have imagined that as young men they would be world famous violinists with best-selling albums and even performing in front of the American President, Barack Obama.

*The two brothers, Tourie and Damien Escobar, were able to use their incredible talents with the violin to avoid the potential adversity that others with their background may have been susceptible to. But they didn't leave their roots behind and soon began to blend the music of their home (pop, rock and hip-hop) with the classical music they were studying at the acclaimed Julliard School in New York City. This unique fusion of genres became their signature and **Nuttin But Stringz** was born.*

Along their journey of success, the boys faced many choices and decisions, but always fell to their violins for support. As teenagers they played on the subways to earn money to help their single mum care for the family, sometimes making almost $300 in only a few hours. Through their continued self-belief, the pair have gone from busking to competing in the television series **America's Got Talent**, featuring on the movie **Step Up** and playing shows with other legendary artists, turning them into highly respected musicians and composers.

Behind their success is a deeper understanding of their purpose as performers and they often take time out to give something back to society. They have worked with numerous charities, especially with young children, in an attempt to encourage others to make strong choices and have the courage to follow their dreams. As Tourie says, "We know it can be hard for kids to be individuals in today's society but we are examples of where being different and following your dreams can get you."

For more about **Nuttin But Stringz** visit www.nuttinbutstringz.com

You may not be able to choose what happens to you, but you *can* choose how you *respond* to it.

Get the Power

When we're faced with a particularly challenging situation we usually respond in one of two ways: positively or negatively. (We've already looked at this in the episode on gratitude.)

If you are a positive person, you are *empowered*. You have an optimistic and upbeat attitude towards life, and are able to make creative choices that help you deal with situations in a positive way. You believe that it is *in your power* to choose the best outcome for you.

A negative person is *disempowered*. They are moaning, groaning, pessimistic people who make unhelpful and negative choices. They believe that they have *no power* to change the way things affect their life.

Think of it like looking through a telescope. If you look through one end, everything seems bigger. Just like being empowered, you can see

Empowerment
Within my reach

things in great detail and can feel that they are within your reach. But if you look through the other end of the telescope, things seem smaller and further away. When a person is disempowered, they can't see all the good stuff in life, and everything feels well beyond their reach.

An empowered person believes:
- I have a choice;
- I can do something about it;
- I will be able to change it.

A disempowered person believes:
- I don't have a choice;
- I can't do anything about it;
- I won't be able to change it.

Which would you rather be?

Matt wasn't much interested in school and, although he always did well in class, he was often bored. To keep himself amused, he used to draw during class. In fact, he got so good at it that he was able to draw without looking – so that the teacher would think he was paying attention. In particular, he liked drawings and liked to tell stories through his drawings.

Matt's parents and teachers suggested that he go to college in order to get a reliable job. Matt ignored them, however, and chose to go to a college that focused on the arts.

He used his desire for writing and drawing to become the editor of the campus newspaper.

*When Matt graduated from college, he moved to Los Angeles to become a writer. There, he had what he described as 'a series of lousy jobs', from washing dishes to gardening, to working at a sewage-treatment plant. Although things were tough, Matt's positive outlook and desire to become a cartoonist brought him the opportunities he needed to become a success: soon, his comic strip, **Life in Hell**, was being published in newspapers and in book form across America.*

***Life in Hell** became a huge success, but Matt was still open to further opportunities. When the comic strip caught the eye of a Hollywood writer-producer, Matt Groening took only fifteen minutes to design the five members of the dysfunctional Simpsons family.*

*The success of **The Simpsons** surprised even Matt. It has won dozens of awards and has even been named the twentieth century's best television series. Just think what would have happened if Matt had been influenced by other people's opinions back when he was in school, or if he had not had the confidence to make positive choices in his life.*

Making Empowered Choices

There are some areas in life that *really* benefit from positive responses to a situation. Three in particular need to be mentioned here:
1. Bullying
2. Diversity, and
3. Self-image.

Bullying

Just like being called names, which we discussed above, being bullied is never a nice experience. Being bullied can make you feel scared, alone or angry, and can even make you physically ill. A disempowered person believes there is no way out of the situation, and that they have no choice but to put up with the hurt they feel. But that's not true! If you are empowered, not only do you believe that everyone deserves to be treated with dignity and respect, but you also know that the way you choose to respond to the situation can help make things better.

Take Action Against Bullying

a. Talk to a friend or an adult whom you trust;
b. Find someone you and the bully can both talk to (a mediator), to help you understand and, ultimately, fix the problem;
c. Have the courage to take action if you see someone else being bullied: bullying stops in 90 percent of cases where a peer intervenes.

Diversity

We all know that everyone is different: being unique is what's great about being human. People are different in what they think and believe, and in what they look like and sound like. We know that people are different based on religion, sexuality, race and disability. But sometimes, when we meet someone who's different from us, we don't know how to react. A disempowered person will only see the negative points of the differences, but an empowered person will embrace the differences and use the experience to understand and celebrate the diversity.

Embrace Diversity

a. *Understand* difference for yourself: don't be influenced by other people's opinions;
b. *Respect* difference: everyone has the right to be different;
c. *Celebrate* difference: enjoy the variety of difference that exists by taking part in events like the Chinese New Year, Diwali or Gay Pride events.

Self-image

Self-image is the mental picture you have of yourself: how you look, and how you behave. Lots of us have a big gap between how we wish we were and how we believe ourselves to be. This gap can make us feel low or insecure, and it can make us doubt our abilities. We call this a negative self-image: 98 percent of fourteen-year-olds have a negative self-image.

As with any area of your life, you have a choice about how you see yourself. If you make the empowered choice to view yourself in a positive way – believing in yourself and having positive thoughts – your behaviour and attitudes will become more positive. Soon you will have a positive self-image that will help you to accomplish all your goals and become a success!

Get Positive

a. Replace negative thoughts about yourself with positive ones: if you have a negative thought, immediately correct it with a positive one;

b. Accepts your mistakes and learn from them;

c. Take responsibility for your own feelings and make positive choices about how you respond to them.

I had always been told that drugs were bad. Drugs were for losers. I had been offered them before when I was at school, but had always said no. None of my close friends took them, and I was never that interested in them. The people who took them were not the type of people I wanted to be.

But in college, it just seemed different. Lots of people were taking them. And they weren't drug addicts, criminals or gangsters; they were ordinary students like me, and they seemed to be having fun. So one day, I took a puff of some marijuana. To be honest, I was so paranoid about what it would do to me that I didn't enjoy it at all.

The next time I was offered some, I just said no. I remember some of the guys laughing at me at the time, so I made up some excuse about having a big game that weekend. They knew I played a lot of sport, so this seemed to work. I didn't lose face; I was still in with the in-crowd.

I was into sports, and having a game became my running excuse for not taking drugs. Eventually, I used this as an excuse not only to refuse the drugs, but even not to go out at all. I didn't want to say no to the drugs, and lose face. Looking back now, I feel so lucky that I had something positive, like sport, to help me focus on what I really wanted.

Some of my friends made different choices. One in particular was short of money; he started to deal drugs to make some extra cash on the side. At first, it didn't seem so bad. He just bought a little extra, and sold what he didn't use himself for a profit.

But then he began to sell more and more. He got in trouble with the police on a few occasions, but it didn't seem to matter to him. *Despite pleas from friends and family, he thought he'd be fine. He seemed to think that dealing drugs was just a temporary thing.*

But it wasn't. Sometime later, he was caught with a large quantity of drugs and ended up spending a few years in jail. By this stage, I wasn't really friends with him any more. We hadn't spoken in years. But when I heard what had happened to him, it really scared me. It had happened so easily. He was a very smart, friendly guy who came from a good family and had lots of potential. It showed that we are either victims or masters of the choices we make.

The story does have a happy ending, though. My friend has started to make better choices. He recently completed a two-year program in an alcohol-and-drug clinic and is starting to get his life back on track. I still haven't spoken to him, but maybe someday in the near future we will be friends again. If it's up to me, I will certainly choose him as my friend again.

Padraig is managing director with
The Super Generation *and co-author of* **Make It Happen**

Press the Red Button ▶

Making Positive Choices

When we are faced with a difficult situation, it is easy to make a decision too quickly or before we have complete information. These decisions are often ones we regret afterwards. However, with our handy Pause, Ponder, Play tool, you can take time out to make sure you can make a positive choice. It's like a remote control for your mind!

1. **Pause**

   Stop to consider the problem, challenge or opportunity, and acknowledge your *true feelings* about the situation, whatever theymay be.

2. **Ponder**

   Imagine a clear space in your mind. This is a quiet, calm environment where you can go to think about the situation. You can imagine different perspectives, and different consequences and outcomes which flow from different decisions. You can view the situation from the magnifying end of the telescope to find a positive solution, or you can make it all seem small and negative. It's your choice.

3. **Play**

   Prepare to leave your clear space, knowing that your choice will be either empowering or disempowering. Make your choice, and take action!

Make the Right Choice

Jenny is being ignored by Helen, another girl at school. She has no idea what she's done to make Helen behave this way, and she's sick of the whole situation. She's tempted to have it out with Helen – even though she knows that they'll get into an argument and may never speak to each other again.

When Jenny gets home, she flops down on the sofa and picks up the TV remote. She presses 'Play' on the remote and begins to watch the film she recorded the night before. But her feelings about Helen just won't go away. She picks up the remote to pause the film: as well as making the film stop, it makes her stop too. As Jenny takes some time out to think about the problem, she realises that it is not making her angry, but miserable and confused. She doesn't hate Helen; she just wants to resolve the situation.

Jenny closes her eyes and creates a clear space in her mind. She remembers the situations she has been in with Helen at school, and tries to see things from different perspectives. She imagines what Helen is going through at the moment, and how she might be feeling. She tests out some scenarios about what she could do next: ignore Helen, confront her in anger, try to talk to her, and so on. She pictures how these situations may end, and tries to find a positive outcome.

Finally, Jenny realises that in order to feel positive about the problem, she needs to talk to Helen to find out what might be wrong. She decides to take action about the situation and not feel bad about it. If she tries to talk to Helen and the situation between them doesn't get better, at least she will know that she has done all she can to resolve the problem.

Jenny comes out of her clear space feeling positive and ready to deal with the problem. She picks up the remote and presses 'Play'. When the film ends, she picks up the phone to speak to Helen and sort things out.

Good choice!

Sometimes our own feelings about a situation are so powerful that it's difficult to step back and see the full picture. When we act from a position of defensiveness or vulnerability, we can often lash out and behave in ways that, looking back, may have been unkind or unnecessary. Although we may get our feelings off our chest at that precise moment, things said or decisions made from a position of insecurity do not always have a lasting positive effect – not least within your own conscience.

We believe that in a situation where you are called upon to make decisions about events or your own behaviour, the best thing you can do it to ask yourself the following question:

'What would the person I want to be do in this situation?'

Devised by the entrepreneur and business coach, Keith Cunningham, we think this is the most important question you can ever ask! It's not asking what *you* would do in the situation, but what an ideal version of you would do. By stepping out of yourself for a few second and imagining how a *perfect* version of yourself would behave, it's amazing the difference you will feel when you come back into your body and make your decision. In some ways, it's like having a guardian angel guiding and advising you how to behave, but don't be fooled: that can make us think there is some other force helping us over which we have no control. We know however, that our power is already within us - all we need to do is stop and listen to it. And the great thing is that the more we visualise and question our ideal self, the more our superconscious realises who we wish to be and helps us to become that person. It's all part of that great journey of success!

Heads or Tails

1. People who succeed are more likely to make decisions slowly and carefully.

2. Good decisions are not unnecessarily influenced by other people's opinions.

3. You may not be able to choose what happens to you, but you *can* choose how you *respond* to it.

4. An empowered person believes:
   • I have a choice;
   • I can do something about it;
   • I will be able to change it.

5. Make good choices about bullying, diversity and self-image – for yourself and for others.

6. Take time out to consider empowering ways to deal with life's challenges: Pause, Ponder, Play.

Up Next: How Good Friends Can Help You Achieve Success

▶ Now and Next 📺

NOW	**Team Game: How true friends can help you achieve success**
NEXT	**Manage Your Thoughts: How tapping into your intuition can have amazing results**

There are two sorts of people in life: those who boost you up, and those who bring you down. And if we don't choose our friends carefully, it's easy to find ourselves spending time with people who have a negative influence on our dreams and desires. Being with such people can make us feel low, miserable and useless. We start to agree with what they say, and to believe that our dreams are impossible and that we won't amount to anything. We call these people dreambusters.

With dreambusters all around us, it's important to have really good friends to support us in achieving our goals. It's also important that you are a good friend, and support others in following their dreams. When you have a good friendship group (even if there are only two of you), you will create a powerful energy between you that will fuel your journey to success.

Reality Bite 🗣️❗

Working together really can create amazing results. In fact there are many things in life that you can't do on your own - like play tennis for example. Music is something that becomes more powerful when there are a group of musicians rather than a solo artist. The blending of instruments really adds to the impact of the music.

Orchestras work together to create and perform music that is full of power and intensity. Most people believe that in order to play in an orchestra you need have great experience with your chosen musical instrument and that it is a difficult feat to take your place as an individual in a huge team of musicians, many playing different instruments and different music to yourself. Imagine the surprise then at the New York Band and Orchestra Festival when the highly esteemed Gold Award was presented to South Pasadena Children's Orchestra.

The competition was made up of senior school orchestras and yet the South Pasadena entrants were from junior school and ranged in age from five to twelve, making them the youngest ever string orchestra to play at the Carnegie Hall. Their age had no reflection on their standard of performance and many of the audience didn't realise they were so young until they stood up to play their final piece.

It just goes to show that belief and a great team can have world record-breaking effects!

What Are Friends For?

Some friends are made by chance, perhaps at school or at a club. These friends are often just there for the good times – for a bit of fun, or to hang around with. These are great friends to have, but they're unlikely to be the type of friend who will be there for you whenever you need them.

Sometimes, however, we begin friendships because we feel drawn to a person in some way. It's as though our superconscious can tell before we can that they will be a good person to be friends with. Real friends connect with each other on a much deeper level, and can enhance our lives in many ways – not least in helping us to achieve our goals.

The strange thing is that our true friends can often seem as though they are not our friends at all. These are the people who will tell us when they think we are behaving badly, or who will have a row with us because they think we are in the wrong. They will tell us the truth, often when we least want to hear it.

True friends may tell it like it is – even if the news hurts. But they are doing this because they support us: they want what's best for us, just as we want what's best for them. Even if a true friend disagrees with you, they will still support your decision, encourage you to achieve your goals, comfort you when the going is tough, and be there to congratulate you when you succeed.

Channel Hop

Poetry Corner

A good friend will tell you what you want to hear.
A true friend will always tell the truth.

A good friend seeks to talk with you about your problems.
A true friend seeks to help you with your problems.

A good friend will be there for you all through school.
A true friend will be there till the day you die.

A good friend brings a bottle of wine to your party.
A true friend comes early to help you cook and stays late to help you clean.

A good friend hates it when you call after they've gone to bed.
A true friend asks you why you took so long to call.

A good friend thinks the friendship is over when you have an argument.
A true friend calls you after you had a fight.

A good friend has never seen you cry.
A true friend has shoulders soggy from your tears.

A good friend doesn't know your parents' first names.
A true friend has their phone numbers in their address book.

A good friend expects you to always be there for them.
A true friend expects to always be there for you.

Encourage Diversity

It's all too easy to look for friends who are just like you, sharing all your views and interests. But just because someone may not think the same way as you do, doesn't mean you won't get on with them. In fact, friends who have a different way of thinking from you can be a good thing when you are looking for new thoughts and ideas. You are more likely to benefit from spending time with a group of people who have different opinions from you than with people who all believe the same things as you. So don't turn someone away just because they don't fit in with your circle of friends: they may have more to offer than you realise.

Friends who have different ways of thinking can be a good thing when you are looking for new thoughts and ideas.

Power Up!

All the things we've mentioned so far can be done by yourself. Alone. But think how much easier they would be if you had a friend to work through them with. Or a *group* of friends.

We've talked about the power of the superconscious, and the way it can affect the energy that surrounds us, to create opportunities that will make positive changes to our lives. When we get together with like-minded individuals, the potential of our superconscious combines with the superconscious minds of our friends to create a powerhouse of energy that will drive us all towards success. It's a bit like a battery: one battery will give a certain amount of energy – maybe enough to power a clock or a torch. But when you combine several batteries together, you get enough energy to do more exciting things, like power a laptop computer or work a remote-controlled car.

As the saying goes: two heads are better than one!

I live in a small town in the midlands. I was about ten when I had a crush on a lad in my class. I didn't think much of it, as I assumed that other lads must feel the same. But when I started in an all-boys secondary school, I began to realise that I was different – though I didn't want to admit it.

In the school, words like 'gay', 'queer' and 'fag' were putdowns and insults. Everyone seemed to have a negative attitude towards homosexuals. I didn't know what to do: all I knew was, that I didn't want to be one!

I did everything I could to 'encourage myself' to be straight, including looking at **Playboy**, imagining that I liked girls, and pleading with God to change me. However, nothing worked. Finally, I admitted to myself that I was gay.

In school, I hung around with a group of lads I'd been friendly with since primary school. One day, one of them told me that his brother was gay. I asked a few questions about my friend's brother: he seemed to have a normal life. He was about to enter college, and it seemed his friends were fine about him being gay. I was so relieved!

After thinking things through for about a month, I decided I would come out. I hoped that I would be able to free myself from my misery. What could be worse than living a lie about who you really are?

So one night, when I was texting my closest friend about girls, I told him I wasn't straight. He wanted to know what I meant, so I told him: I fancy guys. Waiting for his reply seemed like forever, but he was absolutely fine with it, and came around to my house to tell me so in person. Later, I told another of my friends, and he was OK with the idea too. Eventually, all my friends knew about my sexual preferences. No one had a problem with it: they still liked me for who I was.

Coming out to my friends was probably the best thing I have done in my life. I now know that I have real friends, and I am so happy for that. I was so proud of one of them, who stopped an older guy from bullying me in school because of my sexuality. I'm sure we will be friends forever.

Paul is now seventeen and in his final year at school; he hopes to study architecture in college

You've Got to Give to Get

Having a good friend, or group of friends, will bring you all sorts of benefits if you put in the effort to help each other. Helping others might feel like it is not helping you with your goals, but you will find that the more you help other people, the more likely they are to help you when you need support. We've already mentioned that you never get something for nothing. The more you put in, the more you are likely to receive.

'Friendship is like a bank account. You cannot continue to draw on it without making a deposit.'

Nicole Beale

Eco-mind

Here at Eco-mind Limited, we're taking recycling to the next level. Already, people are aware of our limited natural resources and are working hard to maintain and maximise what's left. But what about our personal resources? How can we maximise those?

Eco-mind Limited has developed a new and exciting device that we call the 'Mate-o-mixer'. The Mate-o-mixer works by individuals combining their personal assets with those of their friends to produce a wide range of skills and support. The individual can then benefit from these new assets, as well as their own existing talents.

Assets accepted include:

*   Energy
*   Commitment
*   Challenge
*   Respect
*   Ideas, and
*   Feedback.

Once you have been put through our patented Mate-o-mixer machine, you and your friends will be presented with a box set of beneficial attributes, including:

*   Confidence
*   Skill
*   Experience

- Progress
- Support, and
- Original thought.

If your group of friends would like to benefit from this scheme, call Eco- mind today! Please note: attributes such as anger, resentment, negative thinking and pessimism are not accepted in the Mate-o-meter.

Jordan Romero had a dream to climb the 'Seven Summits' - the highest mountain peaks on each continent (although there are actually eight to climb in total - go figure ☺). In May 2010, Jordan reached the peak of Everest and at only thirteen years old became the youngest person to reach the summit. His final challenge is the Vinson Massif in Antarctica.

The success Jordan achieved was only possible with the support of others. In fact, his homepage holds the slogan: 'Every Step of Our Journey Requires Teamwork.' It's so important it's right there before your eyes.

Without the support of his parents, who train and climb with him, and the guides that help trace the journey to the summit, none of Jordan's success would be possible. Together, however, they are all able to achieve what many may say is unachievable.

For more about Jordan's adventures visit www.jordanromero.com

Don't forget then that success comes in many forms and often requires more than one person to make something happen. It's not a sign of weakness to need others to support you and help you achieve your vision. Who knows, whilst you're at it you may be helping someone else to achieve theirs!

60 Seconds

Team Game

1. A true friend will support you and help you in whatever you decide to do.

2. Our superconscious can often spot a true friend before we do!

3. A group of friends sparks more creativity and solutions than an individual.

4. The more you put in, the more you will get back.

5. Friends who have different ways of thinking can help you develop new thoughts and ideas.

Up Next: How Tapping into Your Intuition Can Have Amazing Results

▶ Now and Next 📺

NOW   Manage Your Thoughts: How tapping into your intuition can have amazing results

NEXT   Talk the Talk, Walk the Walk: How communication is crucial if you want to make things happen

Look into my eyes . . . Make your mind a complete blank . . . You are growing sleepy . . . One, two, three, and you're under!

Most of us associate the idea of thought control with hypnotism and the amusing (for us) and embarrassing (for the person being hypnotised) things that people can be made to do when they are not fully conscious. For example, a hypnotist could make you quack and pretend to lay an egg every time the doorbell rings.

But hypnotism is not all about entertainment. Lots of people visit qualified hypnotherapists who can successfully help them deal with phobias or addictions, such as a fear of spiders, or an addiction to nicotine. All this is done through the power of the superconscious mind.

The Superconscious and Thought Management

We've already talked about the superconscious mind and how it works for or against us, depending on what information we give it. Like a supercomputer, the superconscious is always processing data – in this case, the information we give it through our five senses. If we give it negative thoughts and feelings, it will use these thoughts to influence our desires, and we will become stuck in a pattern where nothing seems to go to plan. But – and this is the fantastic part – if we feed our superconscious with positive thoughts and feelings, the negative thoughts will disappear, and everything will start to work in our favour!

Clever as it is, the superconscious can't cope with positive *and* negative feelings at the same time. So if we alter our behaviour to apply and use positive emotions, so that this becomes a habit, the superconscious will build a barrier to ward off any negative emotions that come your way. Of course, this takes patience and persistence, but in Episode 15 we'll give you some help developing these attributes. The superconscious can't cope with positive *and* negative feelings at the same time.

Sprays an Invisible Barrier that
STOPS ALL NEGATIVE THOUGHTS DEAD!

NEG PRO

With positive thoughts flooding in, your superconscious will begin to work on these thoughts, preparing to help you achieve your goals. By actively working with your superconscious and tapping into your intuition, you can influence and control your inner thoughts, so that your superconscious is *really* listening to your desires, and helping you move further along the path towards fulfilling them.

Reality Bite

Some people begin following their intuition from a very early age. Ingvar Kamprad, who was raised on a small farm in rural Sweden, began his first business venture at the age of five, when he started selling matches to his neighbours. By the time he was seven, he had begun to sell the matches to people in surrounding villages, visiting his customers by bicycle. Soon he expanded his products to include flower seeds, greetings cards, Christmas-tree decorations, pen and pencils. His business was flourishing.

When Ingvar was seventeen, his father gave him some money as a reward for his achievements at school. Ingvar used this money to fund the retail business we now know as Ikea. (The company's name comes from the initials of Ingvar Kamprad, his farm, Elmtaryd, and his home parish, Agunnaryd.)
Ingvar continued to tap into his intuition: he showed great flair

for knowing when to expand and when to focus on selling furniture. Arguably his best idea was to promote the concept of flat-pack furniture so that it could be easily carried home from the showroom in the customer's car. This is still a key feature of the Ikea brand around the world. From the establishment of the first store in 1958, Ikea now has 301 stores in forty countries – and is still expanding.

What is Intuition?

Intuition means 'in to you' in Latin. Now that's not 'in to you' in a 'He's so into you' kind of way, but rather a way of dealing with things from an internal perspective. Some people say that intuition is your spirit talking to you, while others understand it as your superconscious mind calculating what you should do or feel, without your conscious mind being aware of it. It's what we often call our 'gut feeling', and we can use it to help us make important decisions in our lives, as we described in Episode 9.

Intuition is our superconscious working out what we should do without our conscious mind being involved. We can use it to help us make important decisions.

We often get a 'gut feeling' when we're about to make a decision, or if we're with someone who is experiencing trouble and might need our help. We all get great ideas that seem to come from nowhere. These are all examples of following our intuition and acting on instinct. So why not train your superconscious to help you use your intuition? We can do this through altering our state of consciousness, using meditation. We can train our superconscious to access our intuition through meditation.

Reality Bite

Magnus Carlsen was born in Norway in 1990. He began playing chess at an early age and took part in his first chess tournament when he was eight. By the time he was thirteen, he was a grandmaster (the highest chess rating) – and the third-youngest grandmaster in history!

Some people think that Magnus's success is due to his extraordinary talent, but maybe there's more to it than that. As Magnus himself says: 'I spend hours playing chess because I find it so much fun. The day it stops being fun is the day I give up. Without the element of enjoyment, it is not worth trying to excel at anything.'

Magnus succeeds at chess not only because he works hard at the game and enjoys it, but also because he uses his intuition to make the right decisions to win the game. As Magnus's father, Henrik, put it: 'I would not say Magnus is naturally hard-working. In fact, he can be quite lazy at times. But when he is following his intuition and curiosity, there is no stopping him.'

If you find something interesting and motivating, you will succeed because your superconscious will work extra hard to figure out the answers. This is just as important as talent and hard work when it comes to achieving success.

On 1 January 2010, the world chess rankings had Magnus as the world's number-one chess player. At only nineteen years of age, this makes Magnus the youngest number-one chess player in history. Now, how's that for teen success!

Tech Specs

Brainwaves

Depending on our level of mental and physical activity, we have different brainwaves. Our brain pulses and vibrates like everything else in the universe; we can measure this pulsing using an electroencephalograph (EEG). The number of pulse cycles per second determines which of four categories our brain is functioning in.

Brainwave	Cycles per second	Activity
Beta	13 to 40	Day-to-day waking activity

Brainwave	Cycles per second	Activity
Alpha	8 to 13	Relaxed and effortless alertness while awake (light meditation and daydreaming *This is the best state in which to practise creative visualisation and auto-suggestion.*
Theta	4 to 7	Dreaming, creativity and extra-sensory perception. You can train yourself to enter this state at will, rather than just accessing it as part of your sleep pattern.
Delta	0.5 to 4	Very slow wave pattern associated with deep sleep.

In day-to-day activity, we operate on beta waves, but to create an intuitive or meditative state we need to move to alpha or theta waves. But don't worry: it's not as hard as you think!

Meditation, Not Medication!

Meditation can take you to an altered state of mind without using legal or illegal substances. It's safe. It's free. And it really works.

Meditating on a daily basis helps you clear away the stress and tension you experience on a daily basis. Many of us take on more and more stress each day until we feel overloaded; this can even lead to depression. By meditating, we can keep our mind and body relaxed and ready to deal with new challenges. It's a bit like having a dustbin in your mind: it's much nicer to empty it day by day, and keep our mind fresh and clean, rather than allowing everything to rot away in the bin until we can't stand the smell!

 MAKE IT HAPPEN – A Success Guide for Teenagers

Easy-opening flip-top Brain

Empty your rubbish quickly and easily.

When you meditate, you are able to communicate more deeply with your inner self. You can use this state of mind to recognise the negative influences you receive from others as you try to rationalise their beliefs and apply them to yourself. Once you have recognised these negative influences within your superconscious, you can start working to reject them. Most importantly, meditation develops your intuition, allowing you to develop new ideas and creative responses to problems and issues.

It is possible to meditate by using a CD with some gentle classical or instrumental music. The simplest way to meditate is to simply focus on your breathing. Gently bring your mind to your breath. Feel the air as it enters you body and the sensations as it leaves your body. Fully experience what it is like to breath. If you find your mind wandering gently bring your attention back to your breath. As you practice this will become easier and more relaxing. Your mind 'flows' gently and naturally into a different state of consciousness, reducing your cycle of brainwaves moving from beta to alpha or theta, so that you become unaware of what is going on around you and are able to relax completely. It's a bit like daydreaming, where your mind takes time to recharge itself after all the work you put it through during the day.

When you have completed a meditation session, you will feel refreshed and full of a wonderful sense of well-being. So much so that you may soon develop a habit of meditating for a short while every day.

Channel Hop

Mind Lab

'And now we join Professor Mind in the Meditation Lab, where her experiments into the benefits of meditation have produced some exciting results. Professor, please explain your findings to us.'

'Well, it is most interesting that the benefits of meditation seem to be more than just increasing your superconscious's intuition, as we first thought. Take Subject A, for example. He was forever fighting with his brothers over silly things like what television programme to watch or

who was going to do the washing up. Now, with five minutes' meditation a day, he has much better relationships, not only with his brothers, but also with his friends and other family members.

'Next, we looked at concentration. Subject B was finding it hard to study: revising for exams was a particular effort. After meditating for five minutes each day, she has become much more focused and can study for much longer periods of time. We have also found that the results she achieves are greater, and that her brain is functioning at a superior level, compared to its previous state

without meditation. In fact, we think that Subject B will go on to invent some great things.'

'Subject C has found sleeping very difficult recently. Her brain is full of ideas and will not allow her to relax. After meditating, she now enters sleep easily and has much greater relaxation, allowing her to be fully rested for the next day.'

'In Subject D, we have examined the effects of meditation across a longer period of time. Compared to Subject E, who has not been meditating, we have found some interesting results. Overall, Subject D has much better physical, emotional and mental health than Subject E. Both subjects are from the same background, and yet Subject D has far less colds and illnesses than Subject E. He is also much happier and more confident, and deals well with situations that cause stress and tension. Subject E, on the other hand, very quickly builds up anger and frustration, as well as having certain fears and phobias. Watching the two subjects complete the same task shows you

the vast difference between the two.'

'Fascinating, Professor Mind, thank you. A definite thumbs-up for meditation, it seems! Join us next week for some more fascinating studies into the working of the mind.'

The Benefits of Meditating

Overall, there are some great benefits to meditation:

1. Improved interpersonal relationships
2. Improved concentration
3. More confidence
4. Better sleep
5. Sharper brains
6. Greater happiness
7. Better physical health
8. Better mental and emotional health, and
9. Better decision-making and choices.

So it's easy to see why people who meditate, even for only a few minutes each day, have more friends and healthier relationships, and feel a great deal more satisfied and content with their lives, than people who don't. Wouldn't you like to be someone like that?

Press the Red Button ▶

Tapping into Your Intuition

Take five minutes a day to meditate. Find somewhere comfortable, where you won't be disturbed by other people or noise, and put on your CD or MP3 player, with some gentle instrumental music.

1. Set out your intentions

Tell your superconscious why you want to meditate and what you want to achieve from it. If you're not sure what you want to focus on at first, begin with simply focusing on your desire to meditate.

2. Set your posture

Sit on a chair or on a cushion on the floor, as straight and tall as possible. Let the rest of your skeleton and muscles hang freely around this straight-back position. Rest your hands comfortably on your knees or lap, then close your eyes and bring your attention inward, shutting out what is happening around you.

3. Relax deeply

Breathe through your nose, and feel the muscles loosen in your scalp, then move your attention slowly downwards, across your face, relaxing the muscles at the side of your eyes, your cheeks and your mouth. Continue relaxing and softening each part of your body until you reach your toes. By then, you should be completely relaxed.

4. Focus on your breathing

Become aware of your breath as it enters and leaves your nostrils. Count backwards from ten with each breath you breathe out. If your mind wanders, gently remind yourself that you are focusing on your breathing, and begin again.

5. Visualisation

When you reach zero, begin to think about how you will be as you fulfill the goals you have set for yourself. See yourself being successful and happy as you achieve all the things you have planned. Pay close attention to the sights, smells and sounds that are going on around you, and make everything seem bright and vivid. Then, after a few breaths, allow yourself to slide back into full consciousness, and open your eyes.

When you have finished a meditation session, you should feel invigorated and ready to tackle anything – not least the goals you have set for yourself during the course of reading this book!

As you begin to enjoy the sessions, you can increase the time you spend meditating to ten or fifteen minutes. You might like to buy a meditation CD to help you enhance the skill further.

Keep on Dreaming!

Use the following tips to keep your brain in tip-top shape!

- Mediate every day, even if it's only for a short period.
- A few times each day, become aware of your body and breath, and how it changes as you become aware of it.
- Go to a group to meditate with others. Or find a friend who might be interested in meditating with you.
- Use inspiring resources such as books or audio books, which will help you focus your meditation more clearly.

- If you miss a day, a week, or a month of meditating, simply begin again.

Manage Your Thoughts

1. The superconscious can't cope with positive *and* negative feelings at the same time. Thinking positive thoughts will prevent negative thoughts from entering your mind.

2. Intuition is our superconscious calculating what we should do without our conscious mind being involved. We can use it to help us make decisions.

3. Intuition helps you get your 'inner audience' to listen to your desires.

4. It is possible to enter intuitive or meditative states, using different brainwaves, in order to help us focus on our goals.

5. The benefits of meditation include improved concentration, more confidence, better sleep, sharper brainpower, greater happiness and better physical, emotional and mental health.

6. Take five minutes every day to meditate:

   i. set your intention
   ii. set your posture
   iii. relax deeply
   iv. focus on your breathing, and
   v. visualise your goals.

Up Next: How Communication Is Crucial if We Want to Make Things Happen

▶ Now and Next 📺

NOW   **Talk the Talk, Walk the Walk: How communication is crucial if we want to make things happen**

NEXT   **Never Say Never: How it pays to persevere**

If your want to achieve your goals and be successful, you will have to spend a certain amount of time interacting with other people. The better you interact with others, the easier your road to success will be. So let's check out some ways to lift the communication barrier.

Replay 🔄

The better you interact with others, the easier it will be to achieve success.

Talk the Talk

We spend our lives having conversations with other people. Most of us think of this simply as talking and listening, but it's not as simple as that. A parrot may be able to talk and listen, but can it have a conversation?

Sometimes you can have a conversation without any words at all. A simple raised eyebrow can express a question. A shrug of the shoulders can express lack of interest. An extended finger can express . . . well, you know what we mean. The point is, it's not just about talking. When you're communicating with someone, you are *interacting* with them. You are sharing part of yourself with the other person, and they're doing the same with you. When this works well, you feel as though you understand how the other person thinks and feels. We call this *rapport*.

Rapport

When we feel that we have a connection with another person, we are said to be *in rapport* with them. Being in rapport with someone helps us create a harmonious relationship, because mutual trust and understanding comes easily. As we can see things from the other person's point of view, this helps us make them feel comfortable and accepted. It's as though a space is created around you in which you can both be relaxed and open, able to express your views and opinions, while also accepting and understanding the other person's.

Being in rapport with someone helps us see things from their point of view, so that we can make them feel more comfortable and accepted.

RAPPORT
FOR TRUE INTERACTIONS

Often, rapport comes naturally. We might meet someone new and immediately feel drawn to them. You 'fit', so to speak – like a key in a lock. But just because you don't feel that instant connection with everyone, doesn't mean that you can't help it along a bit. Remember, rapport starts (or doesn't) at the very first meeting you have with someone. Before you even open your mouth, people will begin to draw conclusions about you from the way you look, the way you stand, even the way you smell! So, to get the most out of a relationship, it's important to be aware of what you can do to make it go as swimmingly as possible.

Press the Red Button ▶

Create a Good Impression and Establish Rapport

Follow these tips every time you meet someone and want to start a conversation:

1. *Dress appropriately* for the occasion.
2. *Smile* when you first meet the person.
3. Be the first person to *say hello* and *extend your hand*.
4. *Establish eye contact*, and maintain eye contact throughout the

conversation.

5. *Use the person's name* when you are talking to them.
6. Find out about the person before you meet, to see if you share some *common ground* that will make the conversation flow more easily.
7. Do more *listening* than talking.

The Art of Conversation

Most people like talking. We like to talk about what we like and don't like, what we want and don't want. Given an opportunity to talk about ourselves, most of us step up to the mark and get stuck in. But have you ever stopped to think about how talking about yourself makes you *feel*?

When someone takes time to listen to you, it feels good, doesn't it? Being listened to makes us feel valued and appreciated. We know that what we are saying is being taken seriously, and a good conversation can often help us grow in confidence.

An easy way to establish good rapport with another person is to make the effort to listen to what they're saying. It may surprise you to know that listening can take many forms. Sometimes we 'pretend' to listen: we make it look as though we're listening, but really we're thinking about something else, like what we're going to have for dinner, or what we're going to say next. *Pretend listening* doesn't make the person being listened to feel valued and appreciated: quite the opposite, in fact. Most of us can tell when someone isn't really interested in what we're saying: this is a sure-fire way for them to lose our respect.

Active listening, on the other hand, is a better way to do things. An active listener puts all their effort into listening to the other person. They will concentrate on what is being said, and react with interest. When you listen actively, you show that you care about the speaker and respect their opinions. A conversation with at least one active listener has far more potential to be successful than a conversation with two active speakers.

Active listening shows the speaker you care about them and respect their opinions.

Reality Bite

I always found it hard to meet girls. I was never able to talk to them. If I was interested in someone and had the opportunity to chat to them, I would end up talking nonsense and making a

fool of myself. I could never think of
anything interesting to say, and got very
nervous and fidgeted a lot. I began to
think I would never be able to get a
girlfriend.

Help was needed. I went looking for
someone who was good at these things.
I thought of my cousin. He was much
older than me, always had a girlfriend,
and could talk to anyone. So I met him
one day and told him about my
difficulty. He told me not to worry and
said he had the secret. Leaning over, he checked that nobody
else was listening, and said: 'The secret to being a good
conversationalist is . . . talk about what the other person is
interested in!'

'That's it?' I said sceptically. 'How am I supposed to do
that?'

'Ask questions,' was the reply. 'The best way to be a good
conversationalist is to be a good listener.'

I wasn't impressed. There had to be more to it than that.
Surely you needed to tell jokes, know lots about everything, and
have done loads of interesting things. Nevertheless, I decided to
give it a try.

While waiting after school one day, I saw a girl I really liked.
She was beautiful: someone I would never be able to talk to, I
thought. I started to sweat with nerves, but eventually I mustered
up the courage and went over and said hello.

We started to chat, and I asked her about her day. Then
about a teacher she had mentioned who had given her extra
homework. She was angry about that, as she didn't like the
subject. So I asked her why, and she talked about the reasons
she was annoyed. I asked what subjects she liked, and why. I
asked her what she did for fun, and if she had anything planned
for the weekend. The conversation went on and on: I asked, and
she answered. I listened intently; she was a very interesting
person, and I started to understand the kind of person she was.

We spoke for an hour or more, although I spent most of the
time listening, and she did nearly all the talking. The conversation
only ended when she noticed that she was really late to meet
her mother. She said a quick goodbye and rushed off.

The next morning, I met one of her friends on the way to school. She told me that the girl had told her all about me later that day. Apparently, she thought I was really nice and easy to talk to. I couldn't believe it: me, interesting, funny, easy to talk to? It was as though she was talking about a different person!

She had asked her friend to tell me that she would be in the same place after school that day if I was interested in meeting her again. I was, and we had another great chat. We met a lot over the next few days. Eventually, she became my girlfriend.

I was astonished and delighted. My cousin's advice was something I always remember, and practise to this day. If you want to be a good conversationalist, the most important thing is to shut up and listen.

Padraig Lawlor is managing director of
The Super Generation *and co-author of* **Make It Happen**

You Don't Listen Just with Your Ears

Communication isn't just about *what* the person says, it's about *how* they say it. A psychologist called Albert Mehrabian has done some research about how we communicate with each other. He found out that only 7 percent of our communication comes from the words we say! So how else are we communicating?

More than half of how we communicate is expressed through our body language. This means that what we say (our words) needs to match how we behave (our tone of voice and body language), or we will not be believed. It also means that when we are listening to someone, we can express how we feel without actually saying anything, and interrupting their thoughts. For example, if your friend is telling you about something difficult that's happening in their life, you can show you're concerned by tilting your head slightly to one side, or by nodding gently to show that you understand how they feel.

Mirror, Mirror on the Wall ...

When we get on well with someone and have a good rapport with them, we show it through our body language and our tone of voice, by mirroring the other person's posture and intonation. We can even mirror someone by using the same type of language as them. For example, when we are with someone we like, we might match how we are sitting or standing to look like them, or we might start to use the same phrases as them, like 'fantastic' or 'awesome'. When we have a rapport with someone, this happens naturally, as our superconscious tries to show the other person that we like them.

We show rapport through mirroring the other person's posture and intonation.

If you want to create rapport, you can use the technique of *mirroring* to help the other person's superconscious relax and feel comfortable.

They're in Tune

To do this, you need to be aware of the person's body movements, facial expressions, key phrases, and so on, and begin to *copy* them. Do it slowly to make it look natural, but when the person you are talking to moves their arm, say, wait a few seconds, and then move your arm to the same position. To your partner's superconscious, it will seem as though you are agreeing with how they feel. It's like showing that you understand how the other person sees the world. As you build the rapport between yourselves, the mirroring will become more natural, until you are no longer even aware of it!

Press Pause ⏸

Hold the Phone!

But hang on a minute . . . Surely all of this can't work when we can't actually *see* the person we're talking to? Well, kind of. Telephone conversations may seem an impossible way to establish rapport, but that's not actually true. If you are going to have a telephone call with someone (especially someone you don't know), make yourself smile before you say hello.

Try it now. Just sit with a blank expression on your face and say 'Hello' – or, if you're in a public place, imagine saying hello. Now smile and say it again. Notice the difference? Even if you don't feel happy, the smile will make you *sound* happy.

By changing your facial muscles, the smile will make your words seem warmer, and the person on the other end will sense that you are open and friendly, and will feel immediately at ease. So for instant rapport, just add a smile!

Mirroring

To become aware of how people mirror each other, start by watching a television programmes to see if you can spot matching behaviour or posture. Reality programmes offer many genuine examples of rapport and mirroring. Once you've seen how it's done, try the following exercise, designed to help you mirror another person's body language and make them feel at ease when talking to you:

1. Choose a partner to have a conversation with, but *don't tell them* you're going to mirror their behaviour. (If you tell them, at best, you'll make them feel self-conscious; at worst, they'll think you're a weirdo!)

2. Start a conversation about their interests. This will make them feel at ease, as well as getting them to lead the conversation. Make sure you are using *active listening*: respond to their comments by showing you understand what they are saying rather than judging it, and presenting your own opinions. For example, reply with: 'So, what I think you're saying is . . .'

3. As the other person is talking, carefully mirror their posture so that you are sitting in the same way as them. Try not to make it too obvious that this is what you're doing!

4. Once your bodies are in roughly the same position, try to use some of the other person's gestures and phrases.

5. Finally, adapt your speech to mirror the other person, in terms of speed and volume. By this time, you will be pretty much in sync with the other person, and may be doing this without even being aware of it. Once you are completely mirroring each other, you will find that you are even breathing at the same rate! You should feel pretty comfortable with each other by then. How cool is that!

Mismatch!

If you don't believe us about mirroring, try doing the opposite. Next time you have a conversation with someone you know really well, intentionally change your posture, gestures, tone of voice, and so on, so that they don't match. Both you and your friend should notice the result. You might have some explaining to do. Don't say we didn't warn you!

Walk the Walk

Posture is how we stand, and the shape our bodies take. We know that good posture supports our skeleton and our muscles, and helps us be healthy and strong. But did you also know that good posture helps your mental attitude? Believe it or not, it's true.

Our mental state is determined by two things:

1. How we create things in our mind (our representation of reality), and
2. The physical position of our bodies.

Replay

Our mental state is determined by how we perceive the world, and by the physical position of our bodies.

Press Pause

Take a moment to remember a time when someone you knew was feeling a bit down or miserable. Imagine them standing in front of you in this sad, sorry state. Look at how they're standing. They are probably looking down at the floor. Their eyes will be sad and dull, their breathing will be shallow, and their shoulders will be slouched. In fact, they may well look as though you could knock them over with one finger. If you've ever felt this way yourself, you'll know exactly what we're talking about.

Now, think of the most confident person you know. Imagine them standing in front of you now. How do they look? Not slouched and slumpy, certainly! A confident person will have bright eyes and strong breathing. They will be looking straight ahead, with their shoulders back and their head up. Most importantly, they will be standing tall and straight: you definitely wouldn't be able to push them over using one finger!

Try it yourself. Straighten your back and shoulders as you read this right now. Do you feel any different? Now try to feel miserable – but don't move! Go on, try harder. No slouching. No looking at the floor. Look straight ahead, shoulders back, smile . . . and feel miserable. You can't do it, can you? It's physically impossible! When your body is physically positive, your mind has to follow suit. And that's definitely worth remembering.

When your body is physically positive, your mind has to follow suit.

Peanuts

PEANUTS

THIS IS MY "DEPRESSED STANCE"

WHEN YOU'RE DEPRESSED, IT MAKES A LOT OF DIFFERENCE HOW YOU STAND...

THE WORST THING YOU CAN DO IS STRAIGHTEN UP AND HOLD YOUR HEAD HIGH BECAUSE THEN YOU'LL START TO FEEL BETTER...

IF YOU'RE GOING TO GET ANY JOY OUT OF BEING DEPRESSED, YOU'VE GOT TO STAND LIKE THIS.

Love the Lingo

Words are all around us. From the minute we're born, we hear words: 'It's a girl!' 'It's a boy!' We are spoken to and spoken about and, by the time we're around a year old, we are beginning to speak for ourselves. But have you ever wondered about the power that words have?

Press Pause ⏸

Take a moment to think about the impact that words can have on people's emotions. Politicians use the power of words to create speeches that will motivate and inspire whole nations. Imagine how different our world would be if Winston Churchill hadn't said 'We will fight them on the beaches' during

World War Two, or if Martin Luther King had never said 'I have a dream'. Think about how empowered people in the United States, and elsewhere, felt when President Obama said: 'Yes, we can!' On a less serious note, think about the programme *The X Factor*, and the power that music producer Simon Cowell holds when he tells potential future pop stars what he thinks of them . . .

But you don't have to make a speech to use words powerfully. Whenever we make a comment about someone or something, we have the power to influence how the listener feels. If you tell someone you like their shoes, for example, that person will feel a little better about themselves. If, on the other hand, you tell them that you've seen better shoes on your grandma, they're likely to feel a little embarrassed. The power's not in your hands, it's on the tip of your tongue.

Channel Hop

The Two Frogs

Once upon a time, a group of frogs was hopping contentedly through the woods, going about their froggy business, when two of them fell into a deep pit. All the other frogs gathered around the pit to see what they could do to help their companions.

When they saw how deep the pit was, the rest of the group agreed that the situation was hopeless, and told the two frogs in the pit that they were as good as dead. (Some friends they were . . .)

Unwilling to accept this terrible fate, the two frogs began to jump with all their might. Some of the frogs shouted into the pit that it was hopeless, while others told them they wouldn't be in such a terrible situation if they'd been more careful. Even the more caring frogs continued sorrowfully shouted that they should save their energy and give up, since they were already as good as dead.

The two frogs continued jumping as hard as they could. After several hours of desperate effort, they were quite weary. Finally, one of the frogs took heed of the calls of his fellows. Spent and disheartened, he quietly accepted his fate, lay down at the bottom of the pit, and died.

The other frog continued to jump with every ounce of energy he had, although he was exhausted, and his body was racked with pain. Filled with grief for his companion, the other frogs yelled for him to accept his fate, and just die. The frog just jumped harder and harder until – wonder of wonders! – he finally leapt so high that he sprang out of the pit.

Amazed, the other frogs celebrated his miraculous escape and then, gathering around him, asked: 'Why did you continue jumping when we told you it was impossible?'

Reading their lips, the astonished frog explained to them that he was deaf, and that when he saw their gestures and shouting, he thought they were cheering him on. What he had perceived as encouragement had inspired him to try harder, and to succeed, against all the odds.

So, words are powerful – and can be dangerous when they are used in the wrong way. Think before you speak, and you will be able to use your words to encourage other people rather than making them feel bad. It's a special gift we should all try to use more.

Reality Bite

*I learnt to talk at a very early age, and enjoyed nothing more than to natter on all day to anyone who would listen. In fact, my godfather's earliest memory of me is being presented with a shape from a toy shape-sorter, and my eighteen-month old voice declaring: 'This is a **trapezium**!'*

So words were never a problem for me, and my parents encouraged me to learn as many of them as possible. I was soon a little walking dictionary.

One day, when I was about four, we came home from a family trip to the zoo. While my father unloaded the car of all the day's paraphernalia – picnic basket, rug, waterproofs – my mother and I chatted with an elderly neighbour who happened to be passing by. He asked me what my favourite animal in the zoo was. I proudly informed him that I liked the hippopotamus best, before skipping off indoors to play. Looking after me in amazement, the neighbour turned to my mother and said, in his country accent: 'My, ain't she plain?'

My mother was mortified. OK, so maybe I wasn't the most beautiful child on the planet, and I'll never make it down a catwalk, but I wasn't plain. In fact, I was quite cute, in a pigtails-and-glasses kind of way.

Being well brought up, however, my mother didn't question our neighbour, and started talking about something else. It wasn't until some years later that she found out that when he said 'plain', he meant 'plain-speaking', not 'plain-looking'. What my mother had thought was an insult was actually a compliment!

*Xanthe is creative director for **Make It Happen***

Make Your Language Work for You

Like the other habits we've talked about, you can change the way you use language. You see, when you make a comment, you don't only influence the listener, you also influence yourself. When our superconscious hears what we are saying, it believes it to be true. So the more negative stuff you say, the more miserable your superconscious gets. And without your superconscious' support, all the other stuff you are doing to reach your goals becomes less powerful.

Press the Red Button ▶

Power Language

Make your language work for you with the following tips:

1. When you speak, take some time to think about *what* you are going to say *before* you say it. Remember, that even if no one else is listening, your superconscious will be!

2. Use *empowering* language to make you feel positive about life and the situation you are in. For example, if someone asks you how you are, say you are 'great' even if you want to only say you are 'OK'. The more positive your language, the more positive you will feel.

3. Always look for a way out of a negative statement, even if it's just stating the facts. For example, instead of saying, 'the weather is dreadful with all the rain' simply say 'there's been lots of rain'.

4. If you do use a negative statement, immediately rephrase it so that your superconscious gets the new, positive message. This will also help to make positive language a habit. For example, if you say, 'I'm so depressed' change it to 'I'm about to feel much better'.

Use empowering language to make you feel positive about the situation you are in.

Remember, using positive communication will not only make you feel more confident and successful, it will also make the people you interact with feel more positive about themselves. Once you've got some good rapport going, people will be eager to help you put your goals in place!

Talk the Talk, Walk the Walk

1. The better you interact with others, the easier your road to success will be.

2. Having good rapport with someone helps you see things from their point of view, so you can make them feel more comfortable and accepted.

3. Active listening shows the speaker that you care about them and respect their opinions.

4. We show rapport through mirroring the other person's posture and tone.

5. Our mental state is determined by how we perceive the world, and the physical position of our bodies.

6. When your body is physically positive, your mind has to follow suit.

7. Use empowering language to make you feel positive about the situation you are in – even if, at first glance, it seems negative.

Up Next: And Finally, How It Pays to Persevere

Episode 15:
Never Say Never

▶ Now and Next 📺

NOW	**Never Say Never: How being persistent can help you achieve great things**
NEXT	**Over to You: Time to get stuck in and make it happen!**

Ever heard the expression: 'If at first you don't succeed; try, try again'? Well, old-fashioned though this may sound, the people who apply it to their lives are on to something. Life will throw up challenges at every step of your journey to success, but it's how you deal with these challenges that determines whether or not you will reach your goals. The fact that you've made it through to the final episode shows that you already have part of what it takes to do this: persistence.

Everyone who achieves success, without exception, is persistent. To be a success, it doesn't matter *what* you want, but *how much* you want it. If you read this book, and then put it on your bookshelf and go back to your life, no matter how good you think the ideas in the book are, nothing in your life is going to change. However, if you read this book and become *determined* to change your life and achieve success, you will find that things start to happen. You can't become successful by being half-hearted: it calls for full-on, teeth-clenching determination.

Replay 🔄

Becoming a success calls for full-on, teeth-clenching determination.

Will Smith was born in west Philadelphia in 1968. His dad was a refrigeration engineer, and his mum worked as a school administrator. When he was a teenager, he started rapping, and he used this talent to get into the music industry.

By the time Will was twenty, he had won the first of many Grammy awards. Although he was a success, Will wasn't too sensible with his earnings. After spending his money and underpaying his income tax, Will Smith had a $2.8 million tax debt that he couldn't repay. The Internal Revenue Service took many of his possessions, and a portion of his income, until the debt was paid, leaving Will almost bankrupt.

*But Will wasn't going to be beaten. In 1990, he was signed by television company NBC to star in his own sitcom, **The Fresh Prince of Bel-Air**. Will then set himself the goal of becoming 'the biggest movie star in the world'.*

*After studying what made a film a box-office success, Will starred in major releases such as **Independence Day** and **Men in Black**, as well as releasing more hit singles. He has been nominated for four Golden Globes and two Acadamy Awards. More impressively, in April 2007, **Newsweek** declared him to be the 'most powerful actor on the planet'.*

The Chosen Few

Will Smith made his goal come true, but have you ever wondered why lots of people say they have goals they want to achieve, but only a few of them ever actually achieve these goals? Do you think it's because they're luckier than other people? Or is it because they know the 'right people'? Or do you think it's because they deserve it more than other people?

People who succeed are more persistent than those who do not. You may be able to find reasons to support some or all of these suggestions, but the truth is that people who succeed are more persistent than those who do not. When faced with challenges or criticism, most people give up. But those who are persistent will keep going, despite any opposition they may encounter. Take a look at Will Smith's view of persistence:

'I will not be outworked. You might have more talent than me, you might be smarter than me, you might be sexier than me . . . but if I get blocked out, somehow I'm gonna get back in.'

Will Smith

Tech Specs

Chemistry Lab

Napoleon Hill said that persistence 'is to character what carbon is to steel'. Now if you've studied alloys in chemistry, you'll know that carbon is added to iron to make it into steel – a much stronger metal. Take a look:

In the same way, if you add persistence to your desires, you will have the character you need to be successful. Think of persistence as being like the protein shakes bodybuilders use to gain weight and muscle strength: persistence will help make you strong.

Apply persistence to the principles in this book, and you'll be on top of your game in no time!

Cultivating Will-power

People often talk about will-power when they are trying to give something up, like chocolate or alcohol or cigarettes. They'll say things like: 'Oh, I wish I could stop smoking, but I just haven't got the will-power.' And because most people find it too hard to persevere, they give up.

But here's the thing: will-power comes much more readily if you actually *want* to make the change you are trying to bring about. People who succeed at dieting or stopping smoking do so because they *really want to*. And if you really want to do something, finding the effort to persist in spite of challenges is much easier than if you're not that bothered about it in the first place.

Press Pause ⏸

Think about something you don't like to do: tidying your room, perhaps, or walking the dog, or doing your homework. Now think about how you feel when you know you have to do this task. Do you feel as though you've got no energy, or that it's going to take ages, or that you just can't be bothered? How would you feel if, just before you started on the task, a friend dropped by, suggesting you go out? Would you rush off, and leave the job for another time?

Now think about something that you enjoy: going to the cinema, or having a nice meal, or playing sport. How do you feel when you think about doing this activity? Are you filled with enthusiasm and energy? Do you wish you could do it right now? If a friend called round when you were about to do this activity, would you find it harder to stop what you were doing?

Most of us find it far easier, and more interesting, to do the things we *want* to do than the things we *have* to do. And if we like what we're doing, it's much harder to stop ourselves from doing it: the will-power comes naturally. We've said it before, but we'll say it again: if you want to be a success, you need *desire* to fire you up to achieve your goals. (And remember, you can always replay Episode 4 whenever your desire is drooping.)

Of course, there will be times when you find persevering hard. But you don't have to struggle on alone. Tell your true friends what you are working towards, and ask them to help you achieve your desires. Just like trying to lift a wardrobe is much easier when there's more than one of you to do it, working towards a goal is much easier with someone else supporting you.

Reality Bite

Teenager Terri Calvesbert leads a pretty normal life, which is incredible considering a terrible accident left her with 90% burns when she was only two years old. Whilst Terri was asleep in her cot, her mum's discarded cigarette caused a housefire so fierce that when the firemen saw Terri they thought she was just a burned doll.

Since that horrible night, Terri has fought the odds and clung onto life against all expectations. She is permanently disfigured from the fire and has no fingers, nose or hair and only one foot. She has already had more than 60 operations and will continue to need surgery for the rest of her life.

Terri says that when things are down and she needs an extra boost to help her through, it is her dad who supports her and gives her the persistence she needs to keep on fighting. In spite of all that has happened and the pain she has gone through, Terri remains remarkably upbeat and refuses to blame her mum for the tragedy. She accepts the good things in her life with an abundance of gratitude and really is an inspiration to us all.

Where's Your Habit At?

We know that our superconscious works continuously. It's on the go 24/7, processing information and changing things that we do regularly into habits, so that we can do them without even thinking about it. We also know that if we only put an occasional effort into pursuing our goals, we are unlikely to get very far. So here's an idea: cultivate persistence until it becomes a habit. That way, reaching your desires will become much easier. It's like taking out insurance against failure: the habit of persistence will offer you comprehensive cover, to ensure that you achieve success.

Cultivate persistence until it becomes a habit.

Remember, even if you are only taking small steps towards your goal, you are still following your desires. Persistence will work, no matter how many challenges you face, especially if you use the experience to help you reach the next stage in your plans. As in the childhood fable 'The Tortoise and the Hare', 'slow and steady wins the race'.

I always loved sport, and played it often. When I started playing football, I was a defender, but during my teenage years I played as a forward – not for my scoring prowess, but more because of my hard work.

I always worked hard and made sure I was at every training session. I pushed myself during the drills to make sure my fitness was at the highest possible level. Every training session, I gave it 100 percent. Sometimes I made the first team, but often I was a substitute. As I continued to work on my game, I was able to get a consistent place on the team as a forward.

My job was to work hard, tackle, win possession and give

the ball to the players who were best at scoring. I always felt I could score more goals myself, and really have an impact on the game, so, during training, I started to work hard on my goal-scoring. Every day, I would practise shooting, keeping the ball low and getting it into the corner of the net. I hit shot after shot, always focusing on the day I might get the chance to do the same in a game.

In my final year at school, that chance came. We were in a semi-final, and the game was level with only ten minutes remaining. We were playing the champions: we had fallen at this hurdle against the same team the year before. This time, we were determined to win.

The ball was moved down the left wing, and I was running to catch up. Diarmuid got the ball, I shouted for the pass, the ball came to me, and suddenly I found myself running towards the goal with only the goalkeeper to beat. The image of the ball crashing to the back of the net flashed in my mind. I could hear the crowd roar the match-winning goal. I held my breath and struck the ball, hard, low, to the left, and . . . wide of the post. I feel to my knees: I'd missed.

Diarmuid came over and picked me up. I continued to work hard, and thankfully we scored, and went on to win the game. We were in the final, and we were delighted. But something inside me still felt I had more to give. I went back to the training field with even more determination than before.

In the final, we played our local rivals. It was a real grudge match, with both of us desperate to win the cup. More than three thousand people come to see the game, and the atmosphere was electric. The game was fast-paced and hard-fought: there was nothing to separate the two teams. The crowd were on a knife-edge.

My chance came. Jason darted out and won the ball. I shouted, and he passed to me. I shot low and hard. The ball went in! I'd scored! The crowd went wild. I couldn't believe it: my hard work had paid off. We held tight and won the game. We were the champions!

I will remember that experience for the rest of my life. I went *from being a player who could barely make the team and was there just to work hard and tackle, to scoring the winning goal on the biggest day in the school's sporting history. And all because I'd been persistent: I persisted in my training; I persisted in keeping myself in great shape; I persisted in working on the weaker parts of my game. And even when things didn't go my way, I persisted. And because of my persistence, I succeeded, and so did my team.*

Padraig Lawlor is managing director of **The Super Generation**, *and co-author of* **Make It Happen**

Pop Quiz

Answer 'yes' or 'no' to the following questions to see if you lack persistence:

1. Are you unsure what you want, or how to define it? ☐ Yes ☐ No

2. Do you put off doing things and use excuses to explain your procrastination? ☐ Yes ☐ No

3. Are you indecisive and get other people to make your decisions for you? ☐ Yes ☐ No

4. Do you rely on excuses rather than finding solutions for problems? ☐ Yes ☐ No

5. Do you feel you can't be bothered to take on a challenge? ☐ Yes ☐ No

6. Do you blame others for your mistakes? ☐ Yes ☐ No

7. Do you feel that you don't want to achieve your goals badly enough? ☐ Yes ☐ No

8. Do you tend to quit at the first sign of defeat? ☐ Yes ☐ No

9. Do you lack organised, written plans? ☐ Yes ☐ No

10. Do you wish that things would happen, rather than you having to *make* them happen? ☐ Yes ☐ No

11. Are you happy to settle for what you've got rather than wanting something better? ☐ Yes ☐ No

12. Do you look for short cuts to success, and feel let down when they don't work? ☐ Yes ☐ No

If you answered 'yes' to a question, think about why you have that trait, and what you could to do to change it. But don't worry too much: our 'Press the Red Button' section at the end of the chapter will help you become a 'persistence professional'!

Reality Bite

Most people show a certain amount of perseverance. Some of us will give up at a second or third attempt. Some of us will reach ten or eleven. But those people who really make their lives a success never give up. Wilma Rudolph was one of those people. In fact, she persevered through so many difficulties and setbacks that it needs a list to show them all:

- Wilma was born prematurely in 1940, weighing only 4.5lbs. The doctors said she wouldn't make it.
- At age 2 she had measles and mumps. The doctors said she wouldn't make it.
- At age 3 she had scarlet fever. The doctors said she wouldn't make it.
- At age 4 she had chickenpox. The doctors said she wouldn't make it.
- At age 5 she had double pneumonia. The doctors said she wouldn't make it.
- At age 6 she had polio. The doctors said she would live but she would never walk properly.

Wilma and her mother refused to submit to the doctors'

diagnosis (they'd been wrong before!) and for two years they travelled fifty miles twice a week to get the physiotherapy Wilma needed. After that, the physiotherapy was performed at home for four years with the help of her brothers and sisters.

Throughout this the Rudolph family continued to show unfailing persistence that Wilma would walk.

- Age 12 Wilma walked unaided.
  The doctors were astonished.
- Age 13 she ran
- Age 14 she ran faster.
- Age 15 she ran faster again.
- Age 16 Wilma won a bronze medal in the Olympics.
- Age 20 she won Olympic gold medals in the 100m, 200m and 400m relay.

During her Olympic wins, Wilma was hailed as 'the fastest woman in history'. Her achievements and success are certainly impressive. In spite of that, her true achievement was her unfailing persistence - without it, the rest would have been impossible.

Criticism

Perhaps the biggest thing that gets in the way of persistence is *the fear of criticism*. We are surrounded by people who judge what we say or do, or even think. Sometimes, worrying about other people's reactions will make us too afraid to do what we want to do. And once we become fearful, we start to question whether what we thought we wanted is the right thing after all. We ask ourselves questions like:

- What will my parents, friends or teachers say if I do this?
- What will my parents, friends or teachers say if I fail?
- What if I'm not good enough to do what I want to do?
- What if I make a fool of myself?
- What if no one likes me any more?
- What if I've made the wrong decision?

Suddenly, the can's open and the worms are everywhere! It's hard to see why you even thought it was a good idea in the first place! So instead of following our goals and desires, we let other people influence our actions, and we compromise.

MAKE IT HAPPEN – A Success Guide for Teenagers

Fear Factor

Annie's friends thought she was amazing: she wasn't afraid of anything. She would go on the scariest rides at the fair. She would climb mountains without being scared of falling. She would even jump out of aeroplanes – with a parachute on, of course!

Annie, on the other hand, knew the truth. She wasn't afraid of doing scary things, but that didn't mean she was fearless. Quite the opposite, in fact. The thing Annie was most frightened of was criticism. To other people, she seemed like the perfect teenager. She would wash the dishes after dinner, taking great care about getting them clean – worried about her mum criticising her. She would do her homework to stop the teacher shouting at her. She would wear the latest fashions, to make sure that her friends carried on going out with her. And for the most part, Annie was happy. She didn't think about the fact that most of what she said or did was due to what other people thought, rather than what she believed in.

Then, one day, an artist came to visit the school. She saw some of Annie's work and said how good a painter Annie could be if she went to art college. This was great news for Annie. But what would her parents think if she told them she wanted to be an artist and not a doctor, as they wanted? And what would her friends say if she told them she was going to college instead of staying on for the sixth form with them? Annie's heart sank.

Fortunately, Annie's desire to become an artist grew stronger and stronger. She spent more time in the art room at school and began to have more confidence in her work. The harder she worked to build up her portfolio, the more she believed in herself. Eventually, her desire to go to art college overcame her fear of criticism, and she told her family and friends what she wanted to do. And, because she was so enthusiastic and confident, her parents and friends were enthusiastic and confident too! A double win!

Fear has a lot to answer for, but if you can develop the habit of persistence and trust in the power of your desires, you can eliminate the fear of criticism. The important thing is that you believe in your actions and truly desire the outcome. As long as this doesn't involve hurting anyone else or having any sort of negative impact on them, the only opinion that really matters is your own. And if you show other people how much you believe in your desires, you'll find that they start to believe in them too.

I wasn't happy. How could I be? I knew before I even opened the envelope that it wasn't going to be good news. My suspicions were quickly confirmed as I saw all the 'C's and 'D's on the results sheet. I had passed, but I didn't have enough points to go to college. I had worked hard, but I just didn't have what was required. English hadn't been good. Maths was a struggle. Irish was poor. Geography and accounting weren't much better. Overall, my final exams had been a complete flop. The night of the results was hard for me. All my friends were celebrating because they were going to college. I was so jealous. I did what any self-respecting seventeen-year-old would do: I went home and cried.

My folks were great, though. They backed me up. 'What do you want to do?' they asked.

'I'm going back to school!'

That night, I made up my mind: I was going back to school; I would get the grades I needed. I was determined that I would be the first person in my family to go to university.

It was a long summer, and I tried to put things out of my mind. By September, I couldn't wait to get going. I threw myself into my studies. Every day, I worked hard. I went to all my classes; I spoke to my teachers; I handed in all my assignments. The year turned out well. In fact, I really enjoyed it. By the time the exams came round, I was ready!

I have much better memories of the results the second time around: it was early in the morning, and I met the postman and asked if there was anything for me. These were pre-internet days, when you got your results in the post. He handed me a crisp brown envelope. As I tore it open, my hands were shaking, and my heart was beating hard. I scanned the yellow page.

'Yes! It's all good!'

I bolted next door.

'Grandad! Grandad! I'm going to college! I'm going to college!'

He looked at me proudly, and beamed. 'I didn't think you'd do it, but you toughed it out. Well done, young man! Persistence is a great thing! Persist, and you will succeed!'

*Ray is an entrepreneur and trainer with **The Super Generation***

Develop Your Persistence

Use these six steps to help you develop your persistence into a habit. We've already discussed each step, so, unless you're reading this book backwards, you should already have a good idea of what each point entails.

1. ## Purpose
   Know *exactly* what you want, and have a strong motive to achieve it (Episode 6).

2. ## Desire
   Keep your desire built up, so that it is easier to be persistent (Episode 6).

3. ## Self-belief
   Trust in your ability to carry out your plans and achieve your desires. Have the confidence to ignore negative and discouraging influences that may distract you from following your path to success (Episode 3).

4. ## Plans
   Have *definite* plans that you can follow, even if they seem impractical (Episode 7).

5. ## Support
   Use your understanding and sympathy towards others to help develop patience and persistence. Find like-minded friends who will encourage you to follow your plan to achieve success (Episode 12).

6. ## Will-power
   Use your concentration and determination to develop your will-power until it is so strong that it becomes a habit.

Listen Up

'If you challenge yourself, you will grow. Your life will change. Your outlook will be positive. It's not always easy to reach your goals, but that's no reason to stop. Never say die. Say to yourself: "I can do it. I'll keep on trying until I win".'

Richard Branson

Never Say Never

1. Becoming a success needs full-on, teeth-clenching determination.

2. People who succeed are more persistent than those who do not.

3. Persistence makes you *stronger*.

4. Persistence will come naturally if you are *passionate* about your goals.

5. Cultivate persistence until it becomes a *habit*.

6. If you don't believe in yourself, no one else will either.

7. Use *purpose, desire, self-belief, plans, support* and will-power to help you build up persistence.

And Finally: Over to You

Over to You...

You've now seen the whole series, and have all the skills at your fingertips to start making things happen in your life. But before we leave you, we'd like to remind you of the main points that will help you achieve success:

Episode 1 — Your superconscious will work for you to create whatever you believe in. Believe in the positive: get positive results. Believe in the negative: get negative results.

Episode 2 — Dream big: your only limit to success is your own imagination. Don't be afraid to play a big game, but keep your life in balance.

Episode 3 — Anything is possible if you have a positive self-image and empowering thoughts.

Episode 4 — You have to strive for success, keep positive and make your superconscious success-conscious. If you can imagine it and believe in it, you can *achieve* it.

MAKE IT HAPPEN: The SUPER System of Success

Episode 5 — **SEE YOUR SUCCESS:** Create a personal vision statement to remind you what you want out of life and to get your superconscious ready to make it happen.

Episode 6 — **UNDERSTAND IT:** Desire, purpose and passion will give you the power to achieve. Failure is just a temporary setback on your journey to success.

Episode 7 — **PLAN YOUR PATH:** Use goals as stepping stones towards your vision. Make them *SUPER*: Specific, Up to you, Positive, Environmental and Recordable. Keep them on goal cards, but only do the most important two or three at a time.

Episode 8 — **EXECUTE & REWARD:** Create an action plan to help you make progress towards your goals. Change negative habits into positive ones, and *get started*.

Episode 9	Cultivate an attitude of gratitude, and you will always see more solutions than setbacks. You'll also have more energy and better mental, emotional and physical health.
Episode 10	Strengthen your self-belief through affirmations and visualisation. Get rid of your inner doubt.
Episode 11	Make empowered choices, and don't be influenced by other people's opinions. You may not be able to choose what happens to you, but you can choose how you respond to it.
Episode 12	A group of true friends will provide you with invaluable support as you follow your goals. But remember: the more you give to them, the more you will get back.
Episode 13	Help your superconscious listen to your intuition by making time each day for meditation. You'll feel better, too!
Episode 14	The better you interact with others, the easier it will be to achieve success. Learn skills to build rapport, such as active listening and matching/mirroring.
Episode 15	You need persistence to succeed. Keep trying, and you will achieve your dreams – we guarantee it.

And there you have it! A step-by-step plan to help you start making it happen. We hope you've found the book interesting, and that it will inspire you to go on to do great things.

What you decide to do next is up to you . . .